I0539150

TO THE EDGE OF
EVEREST
ALTITUDE ADJUSTMENT AT 18,000 FEET

DUANE A. KINGHORN

TIGER SHARK
MEDIA USA

TO THE EDGE OF EVEREST: ALTITUDE ADJUSTMENT AT 18,000 FEET

by Duane A. Kinghorn

Copyright © 2025 Duane A. Kinghorn. All Rights Reserved.

All rights reserved. Published in the United States by Duane A. Kinghorn. This book may not be reproduced, transmitted, or stored in whole or in part by any means, including graphic, electronic, or mechanical without the express written consent of the author or publisher except in the case of brief quotations embodied in critical articles and reviews. Unauthorized reproduction of any part of this work is illegal and is punishable by law.

Written by Duane A. Kinghorn

Photos & video by: Duane A. Kinghorn, Beth, Auggie and Tyler Cipollini

Cover & interior design by Krystal Harvey // Tiger Shark Book Design

www.tigersharkbookdesign.com

Some images used for design courtesy of various Freepik.com artists

ISBN: 979-8-218-85799-8 (Paperback)
ISBN: 979-8-218-85800-1 (Hardcover)
Kindle Version available

Published by:

DUANE A. KINGHORN

Howell, NJ

Email: rdmking@aol.com

YouTube Channel: @ DK Everest Base Camp Expedition

PRINTED IN THE UNITED STATES OF AMERICA

FOREWORD

It was July 2023 when I was asked by Beth and Auggie Cipollini if I was interested in joining them on a once in a lifetime trek to the peak of Mount Kilimanjaro in Tanzania, Africa. Without hesitation I said count me in and then immediately got off the phone and googled Kilimanjaro to see exactly what I got myself into, including where Kilimanjaro was located! I started to do further research, which included watching videos to learn as much as possible about what was needed to ensure a successful trip… physical conditioning, clothing requirements, medical needs (vaccines), etc. The more I learned, the more excited I got and was somewhat anxious as well. Also, needed to tell Eileen and family what I was planning and the commitment I had just made. They were excited for me and at the same time stunned that I would take on this adventure with minimal knowledge and zero hiking experience.

Later that summer we found out that my son and his wife (Ryan and Nicole) were expecting their first child, with the due date a few days after we returned from Kilimanjaro – last week of January, 2024. My initial plans were to continue with this journey, however once we learned that I would be required to quarantine for a minimum of one month due to the potential of contracting various diseases (e.g. Malaria, etc.) in this part of the world, it became prudent that I inform Beth and Auggie that it would not be wise for me to take this risk at this time. I was disappointed that I would not be able to make this trip, but at the same time becoming a grandfather far outweighed anything else and being there for Ryan and Nicole made this an easy decision!

When I told Beth and Auggie and our cousin, Bobby Horan that I could not join them, I could tell they were disappointed, but clearly understood the reason why. However, I did say that if they ever take another trip like this, please consider me, I would be all in. They returned from Kilimanjaro so energized and proud of their accomplishment, with stories fitting of a once in a lifetime adventure, but I did not get a sense that they were in a hurry to try something like this again anytime soon. Well, all the challenges associated with a trek of this magnitude quickly wore off and they were eager to take on the next adventure…Everest Base Camp (EBC)! Within 3 months of returning from Kilimanjaro I received the call to see if I was interested. I immediately said yes and was all in from that day on, no turning back now, Everest here we come!

As a novice, I clearly had a lot to learn and needed to get up to speed quickly on preparation for the trip to Everest that was less than 6 months away. Beth did an amazing job identifying the trekking company (Magnificent Himalayan Treks) and all the travel arrangements that would take us from Miami, Florida, to Doha, Qatar, to Kathmandu, Nepal and back.

Beth and Auggie also helped with identifying the clothing and supplies I would need, joining me on my first of three different trips to REI Co-op. $2,500 later I was ready for any conditions that Everest would throw our way! Also, on one of the trips to REI, Eileen and I met an employee who had recently trekked to Everest and provided us with real life, first-hand knowledge on what to expect, which her advice turned out to be spot on!

Eileen's help was also invaluable in preparing for the trip, as she did a lot of the needed research on what the conditions would be like, including watching countless videos and following numerous EBC blogs. I must admit that I was not all that interested or maybe just in denial of what was in front of me, either way Eileen knew exactly what I was getting into! Eileen was also helpful on some of the shopping sprees, I had enough protein bars, medicine, toilet paper, underwear and socks for everyone on our team and then some!

The rest was up to me to get mentally and physically prepared for what was to come! The mental part was easy, I already made the commitment and for those that know me, once I do that there is no turning back. I also had Ellen Zimmerman (aka motivational coach) whispering in my ear to keep reminding me of that one! The physical training really got going 3 months prior to leaving. This primarily included running a few days a week and hiking the Manasquan Reservoir 2-3 days a week, with my backpack full of 5-6 water bottles and some snacks. In preparation for EBC, the team did go on one serious hike together to Mount Tammany along the Delaware Water Gap in Northern NJ, elevation 1,527ft. Although the elevation was minuscule in comparison to the 18,000ft EBC trek, the fact that a 7-mile trek turned into 14 miles (due to a wrong turn), was good preparation.

As I embarked on my trip to Mount Everest, I cannot begin to tell you how excited I was to experience this next challenge and the anticipation of so much uncertainty that was ahead of us. Some have asked me if this was a bucket list item or a trip of a lifetime? For me it was neither, honestly never on the bucket list, just an opportunity and challenge that I could not say no to.

I have met some very interesting people and have had amazing experiences over 50 years of working. However, since I retired, I felt there was much more out there to experience and going to Mount Everest was just another one of those journeys! Also, at age 64, I figured the window for these types of challenges are slowly starting to close, so now seemed like the best opportunity.

I am dedicating this book to our family, Eileen and my single most important accomplishment! Through thick and thin we have been together for over 35 years, creating a loving legacy, our family! Our love created three wonderful sons, all different in many ways, but with the same caring, smart, hardworking, and loving traits that we imagined when we began our family. Eileen is an amazing mother, daughter, sister, wife, teacher, and friend to so many and has been my best friend through it all!

Ryan, as our first child had to pave the way for his brothers, being the role model, experiencing all our new parenting mistakes and smothering, even having to learn about "life" from his stumbling father! But he persevered through it all and what an amazing man he has become. His smile as a baby was contagious and loveable. Watching him become an incredible athlete and competitor, giving back to others through all his charity work, graduating high school with honors and going on to graduate from college with his Masters was just the start. After graduation he became a teacher, bought his first home, found time to add realtor and college professor to his resume. He is a loving husband and now father to our precious granddaughter Mila, this is just the tip of the iceberg in what he has accomplished in his short life. We could not be prouder of him!!

Drew is our middle child and with that comes a lot of abuse as one of a kind. There can only be one middle child and he broke the mold in so many ways! From the day he was born he was so full of energy, always curious, full of life, laughing and smiling. We are so proud of him and all the firsts he has achieved, from taking steps at 8 months, climbing out of his crib at a year old and somehow getting to the top of the refrigerator as a toddler. Becoming a 3-sport athlete in high school, being on a game show and the team bringing home a win. First in the family to graduate as a civil engineer building bridges and tunnels and before that million-piece roller coasters. Being the smartest in the room, saving us all from the many technology hurdles encountered, the list goes on! Drew has also become an amazing man and husband and I know for sure that he will be an even better father!!

Matt, as the last child had to endure living up to the first two, who were overachievers in everything they did, not an easy thing to do. It could have gone many different ways, but as he does with everything he touches in his life, he perseveres and comes out on top! He has many friends and admirers. He has such a special way of connecting with people and making everyone he comes in contact with feel special. His unique personality was visible from the first day we bought him home and Drew sent him flying in his car seat.

He is always enthusiastic and positive with everything he does, wanting to be the best in every sport and games he plays, including baseball, basketball, golf, and even a few party games, like beer pong! We are so proud of him and the man he has become: graduating from high school with honors like his two brothers before him, selected as senior prom king, graduating from The College of New Jersey as president of his class and becoming one of the youngest senior vice presidents at a major financial institution.

We are also blessed to have three amazing daughter-in-law's, Nicole, Taylor, and Sylwia, that we are very proud of and love very much!! They all have the same core values and loving traits, with their own unique personalities, talents and caring characteristics that make our family complete!

NAMASTE!

MY FAMILY

AN IMMERSIVE JOURNEY

I have organized our journey in chronological order, from the time we left the US, to days trekking to Everest Base Camp, until we completed our journey flying back to the US.

Throughout our story I also utilized:

- YouTube Videos
- Facebook posts/comments, and
- WhatsApp chats to further bring to life what we were experiencing in those moments.

Our Everest Base Camp Expedition team included Beth, Auggie and Tyler Cipollini of Fort Lauderdale, FL and myself, Duane Kinghorn of Howell, NJ. We were also assisted by two guides, Ishwor and Sanket and two porters, Sandesh and Sabin, all of Nepal.

Hope you enjoy coming along on our adventure!

> "
> *So impressive! God bless you for such an accomplishment, truly amazing. You have a beautiful family…they are so fortunate to have you as their figurehead.*
>
> -ROB C.

CONTENTS

✻ Enjoy the short videos posted throughout the book by accessing the QR codes. Please visit my YouTube Channel **@DK Everest Base Camp Expedition**. Under videos click "Oldest" and the videos will be in book order.

*THE EBC TEAM

FROM L-R: Auggie, Tyler and Beth Cipollini, and Duane Kinghorn

CHAPTER ONE

*MOUNT EVEREST BASE CAMP (EBC) PREPARATION

3 to 4 times a week I would put on a heavy backpack and hike the 5-mile **Manasquan Reservoir**. Additionally, I would run 3 to 4 miles twice a week and also got in an occasional bike ride.

Whenever we were in **Ocean Isle Beach, NC**, I walked the length of the island and back – approx. 7 miles each way… not a bad place to train!

During the summer of 2024, we did get in one serious hike that took us to **Mount Tammany**, located near Pahaquarry, NJ (Elevation 1,527ft, compared to EBC 17,598ft). During the hike, Kelly, Tyler's cousin and roommate, joined us. Just like Tyler, she was so much fun, and we were glad to have her on what was my first official hike and only mountain hike before EBC trek!

This is generally considered a challenging route, taking an average of 3 hours to complete. However, that day we decided to take a different route, which took us approx. 7 miles in the wrong direction, along a secured reservoir enclosed by a fence. This resulted in a 14-mile hike, doubling the miles originally anticipated for the day! At the end of the day, it felt great that we were able to go the extra miles, not knowing what was ahead of us in Nepal!

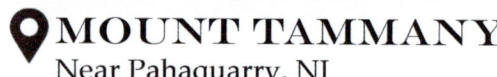
MOUNT TAMMANY
Near Pahaquarry, NJ

Making sure we had the right gear for the EBC trek was critical, ensuring an enjoyable and safe adventure! Gathering gear started with my first trip to REI with the assistance of Beth and Auggie. $2500 later I was prepared and ready to go!

REI CO·OP®
3371 US Rte. 1 #34
Lawrenceville, NJ 08648

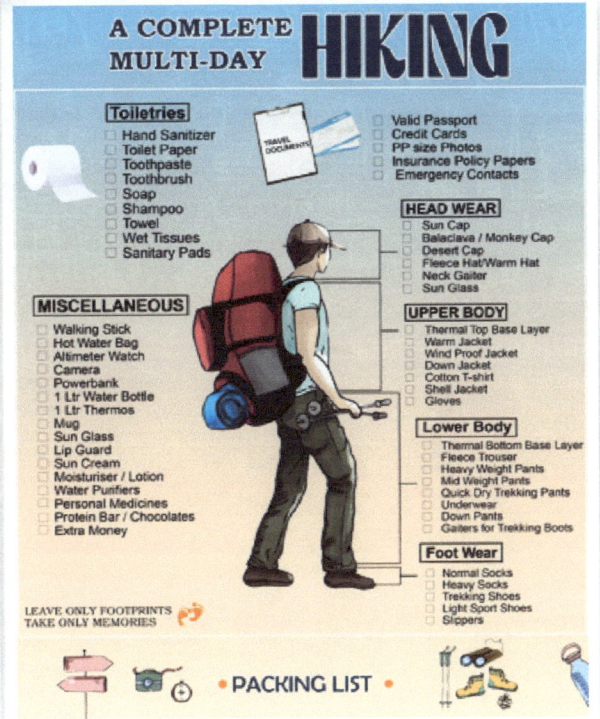

THE CASE OF THE MISSING "MURSE …"

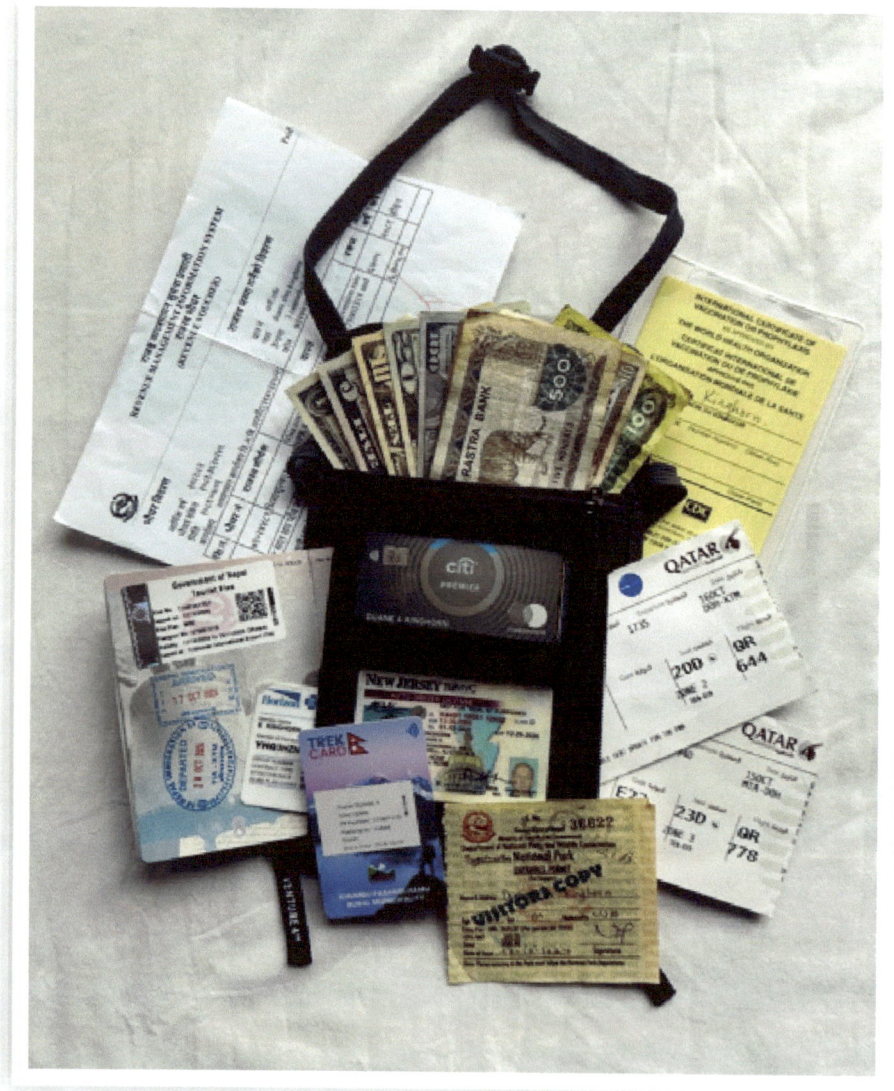

This is known as the **"Murse"**, as Tyler affectionately named for a man that carried a purse during our expedition. I was told early on by Auggie that this would be the most important piece to keep on me at all times, "never let it out of your sight for a minute!"

The murse included critical information that would be needed at every stage of our trip. Contents included, passport, visa, plane tickets, credit card, money (both US Dollars and Nepalese Rupees), drivers license, vaccination cards, etc.

There was only one time that I misplaced the murse and when I did, panic set in! We were staying at the village of Dingboche, just had breakfast and we were getting ready to start our trek for the day. As I always did before I put my backpack on, I would check to make sure my murse was in the front pocket, but this time it wasn't and the zipper to the front pocket was open. My heart rate shot up, I could feel my chest pounding, and of course, thinking the worst had just happened!

For the next 5 minutes I ran all over the place, recalling all my prior steps that took me back to my room, the bathroom across the courtyard and back to the teahouse and nothing.

When I stepped outside to join the team and told them what was going on, there was Auggie holding up my murse and said "are you looking for something?" You can't imagine how relieved I was and that led to a good laugh by all!

What had happened…during breakfast I put my murse into the front pocket of Auggie's backpack, we both had the exact same pack, color, make, etc … *what a relief!*

CHAPTER TWO

*MOUNT EVEREST DEMOGRAPHIC INFORMATION

A little over a week before we left to begin our trek to **Mount Everest Base Camp**, this was the scene at **Gorak Shep**, the village before EBC. Luckily, the poor weather conditions broke and the torrential rains at the lower elevations, mud slides and blizzard conditions at higher elevations cleared just in time for our expedition.

Our goal was to trek to Base Camp 1 depicted at the bottom of this map. I would highly recommend watching the movie *Everest* on Netflix to fully understand the gravity and danger associated with the remaining 5.5 miles to the summit. **Lhotse** is the second highest mountain surrounding Everest at 8,516m (27,939ft), and is where Camp IV is located.

Well, this sucks. It's supposed to be the dry season! 😃

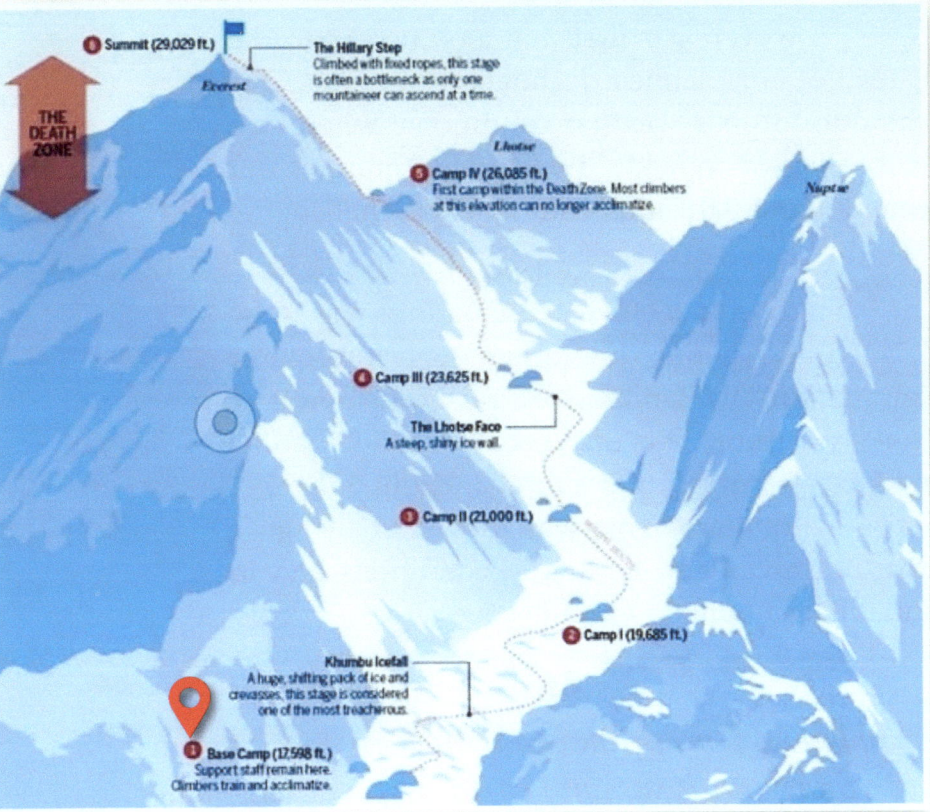

*OUR TREK

There are two options to get to **Everest Base Camp**: we choose trekking vs. a direct helicopter flight tour. This allowed us to experience the full challenge of the adventure to base camp and enjoy and explore the Himalayas.

The trek usually starts from Lukla, and from there, it takes 8-10 days to reach Everest Base Camp, including two acclimatization days at Namche Bazaar and Dingboche.

However, our first day took us to **Surkhe** instead of our planned destination of Lukla. This was due to poor weather conditions, where our helicopter was quickly diverted ten minutes out from landing – this made for an extra challenging Day 1!

Starting our hike to Pakding was now delayed by 5 hours, due to late departure out of Kathmandu and landing several hours south of Lukla at Surkhe. This unexpected location had us trekking several hours more, including over 2 hours in the dark. This was further challenging with no moonlight, in cloudy conditions and in unfamiliar mountain terrain!

“

Thanks for any news, would love to be there but it was never on my agenda.

–CECELIA K.

(89 years old)

SOURCE: Sublime Trails, Trek, Tour, Climb

MOUNT EVEREST IS BETWEEN CHINA AND NEPAL

Mount Everest is the world's highest mountain and part of the Himalayas of Nepal, standing at 8,848m (29,028ft) above sea level. Everest Base Camp is one of two base camps on either side of Mount Everest. **South Base Camp** is located in Nepal at an altitude of 5,364m (17,598ft) and **North Base Camp** is at 5,150m (16,896ft) in Tibet. These camps are primarily used by mountaineers to ascend and descend the World's highest mountain. The Everest Base Camp Trek on the Nepalese side (South side), is one of the most popular trekking routes in the Himalayas, and the destination of our trek.

Nepal's Everest Base Camp is inside Sagarmatha National Park situated in the Solu Khumbu District in the east part of the country. Most of the Everest Base Camp Trek, which starts in the mountainside town of Lukla and ends at base camp, is also inside Sagarmatha.

SOURCE: Tidy Himalaya, Trek & Expeditions

*TERRAIN OVERVIEW

The trek covers approximately 130 kilometers (round-trip) and typically takes about 12-14 days to complete. While the daily distances may not seem extreme, the high altitude and rugged terrain make it physically demanding.

*TERRAIN OVERVIEW

We encountered a mixture of steep uphill climbs, rocky paths, and occasional descents. The terrain is varied, and while the lower elevations may feature forests and rivers, the higher regions are much more barren and exposed to the elements.

*KEY POINTS TO EXPECT

- **Altitude** – The trek usually begins at Lukla, around 2,800 meters (9,186ft) and reaches a maximum altitude of 5,364 meters (17,598ft) at Everest Base Camp. Our trek started south of Lukla at Surkhe, due to poor weather conditions requiring our flight to be diverted.

- **Daily Hiking Hours** – Typically, you'll hike for 6-7 hours per day, with plenty of breaks to acclimatize and take in the scenery.

- **Teahouses** – Accommodations along the trek are provided by small teahouses, which offer basic lodging and meals. These are usually comfortable but simple in the lower elevations, don't expect luxury, and more primitive as you get closer to base camp.

- **Oxygen Levels** – As you ascend, oxygen levels decrease, which makes breathing harder and physical exertion more difficult. This is why acclimatization days are vital during the trek.

*EMOTIONAL AND PHYSICAL CHALLENGE

For many trekkers, the journey is as much a mental challenge as a physical one. The long days, harsh conditions, and the sheer elevation gain can test your resilience.

However, the sense of accomplishment when you reach Everest Base Camp makes every step worthwhile. Experienced moments of awe, difficulty, and exhilaration as we made our way through one of the most iconic trekking routes in the world.

HOW DIFFICULT IS EVEREST BASE CAMP TREK?

SOURCE: THIRD ROCK Adventures, Everest Base Camp Trek: Your Ultimate 2025 Guide

Everest Base Camp Trek difficulty level is moderately challenging and equally rewarding. Basically, the trekkers will hike on average 6-7 hours per day with a light day pack. The trekking route involves rocky terrain, steep uphills, and downhills. So, it is essential to be in good shape and health. Physical exercise such as jogging, swimming, cycling, hiking, etc., will help to build stamina.

However, novice trekkers with average fitness levels can complete this trek, but those who are physically fit can enjoy it more. Previous trekking or hiking experience will be a bonus point, but minimal technical experience and mountaineering skills are necessary for this trip. Also, people with medical issues such as heart, lung, and blood sugar should consult with their doctor before booking the trek.

Since the EBC trek is a high-altitude trek, some people may feel the symptoms of **Altitude Mountain Sickness (AMS)**. Some common symptoms of AMS are nausea, headache, dizziness, shortness of breathing, increased heart rate, etc. If you get the symptoms of altitude sickness, you need to take it seriously; otherwise, your life could be in danger. Some common preventions against AMS are drinking lots of water, ascending slowly, acclimatizing properly, getting plenty of rest, and consuming enough food. Also, after feeling the AMS symptoms, it is recommended to descend to lower altitude immediately.

Although we all occasionally experienced minor altitude sickness symptoms throughout the trek...our vitals, measured by our oxygen levels and heart rate, were excellent. We took these measurements several times each day and became even more disciplined, checking our vitals regularly as we reached higher altitudes.

DANGERS ASSOCIATED WITH
CLIMBING MOUNT EVEREST BASE CAMP
SOURCE: The Himalayan Database

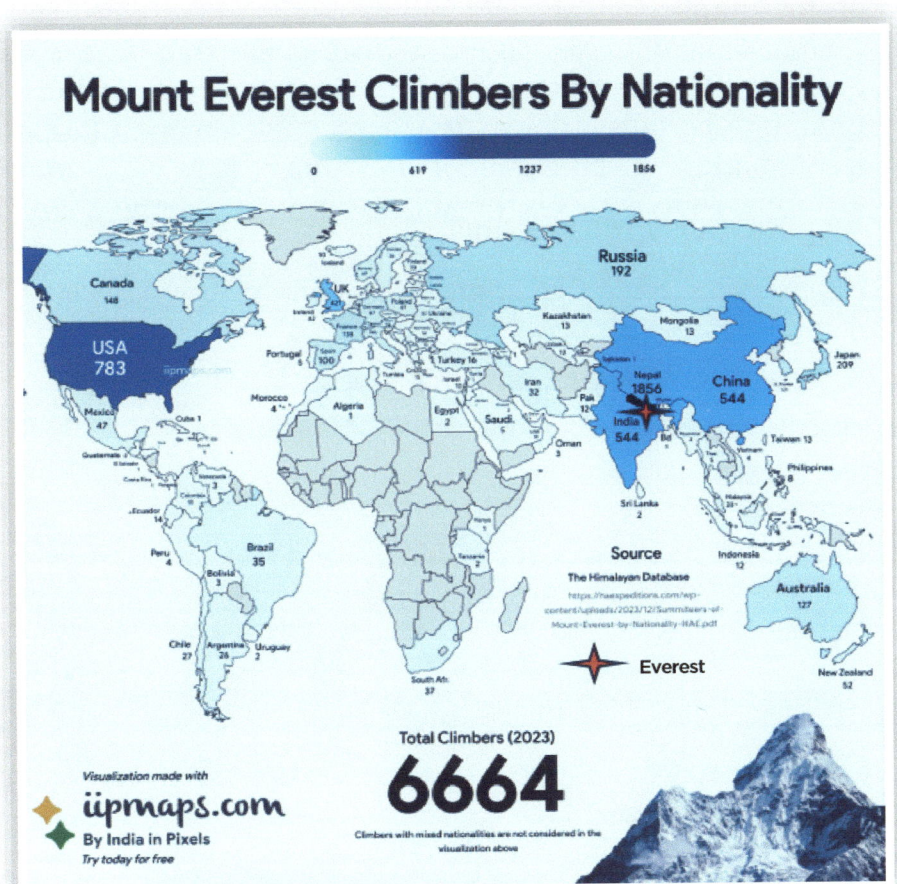

Mount Everest Climbers By Nationality

Total Climbers (2023)

6664

Visualization made with
iipmaps.com
By India in Pixels
Try today for free

Climbers with mixed nationalities are not considered in the visualization above

*MAP REPRESENTS:
Nationality of all climbers who summitted
Mount Everest from 1953-2023

Have people died while climbing Everest Base Camp? Yes, however, the death rate is low compared to summiting the mountain:

ESTIMATED NUMBER OF DEATHS

Estimated number of deaths on the Everest Base Camp Trek range from 12-15 per year, out of approx. 40,000 that attempt the climb. Approx. 70% (28,000) are successful.

CAUSES OF DEATH

Most deaths are due to altitude sickness or underlying conditions that are made worse by the high altitude.

NOTABLE INCIDENTS

- 2014 avalanche: An avalanche on April 14, 2014, killed 16 Nepali team members.

- 2015 earthquake: A 7.8 magnitude earthquake on April 25, 2015, triggered an avalanche that killed 19 people at base camp.

- 2024 deaths: In 2024, 9 climbers died or went missing, down from 18 in 2023.

The **cost of trekking to Everest Base Camp** is dependent on the number of travelers, number of trekking days, and services/amenities you opt for during the trek. The cost generally lies between $1,100 to $4,500, which includes trekking permits, domestic flights (Kathmandu-Lukla-Kathmandu), a professional trekking guide, a porter, accommodations, meals (breakfast, lunch, and dinner), etc.

The premier package to include the Everest Base Camp Trek with a return helicopter flight, will cost a little higher than the standard package.

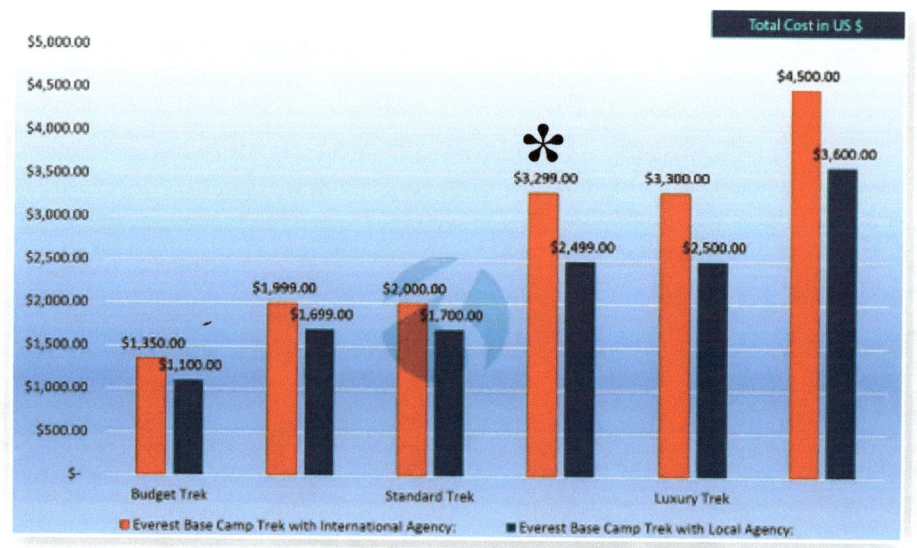

You must get travel insurance when trekking at a higher altitude. We did for our trip. Everest Base Camp Trek is a high-altitude trek that takes you to an altitude above 5,000 meters (16,400ft). A hike can be hazardous, and you can face unfortunate consequences during the trek. Travel insurance is essential if you plan to trek to base camp.

While trekking to the base camp, you might face serious problems such as altitude sickness, injuries, harsh weather, and flight cancellation. Travel insurance will give you peace of mind.

You also need to purchase trekking travel insurance, with helicopter rescue as well. Most importantly, make sure your travel insurance coverage is up to at least 6000 meters (19,700 feet), as you'll be spending at least 3-4 days over an altitude of 5000 meters.

CHAPTER THREE

*EVEREST BASE CAMP ADVENTURE BEGINS

On October 14, 2024, I left Atlantic City, NJ on Spirit Airline for Fort Lauderdale, FL. As I flew into Fort Lauderdale, I was full of anticipation and excitement for what the next few weeks would bring! We had a nice relaxing day, enjoyed dinner on the bay, organized our gear and got a good night sleep for our next round of 20 hours of flights – final destination **Kathmandu, Nepal!**

Stayed at Beth and Auggie's home, Fort Lauderdale, FL., with magnificent views of the Atlantic Ocean!

They are going where?

During our 15-hour flight from Miami to Doha, I was looking at the interactive map on the plane, which provides altitude, speed, ETA, etc., and I noticed location of our plane flying between Israel and Iran. A few weeks before, Iran had bombed Israel and it was expected that Israel was going to retaliate any day. This certainly did not give us an easy feeling as we crossed right between the two countries on our way to Doha.

I also noticed that the map did not include Israel (see map below), but did include the Palestinian Territories. I thought that was odd, but when we landed, I googled and found out that the country of Qatar does not recognize Israel as a state. Since we were flying Qatar Airways, there was my answer.

According to a WSJ article dated Nov. 23, 2024, an average of 162 missiles have been fired each month in 2024 compared to 10 per month in 2023. Missiles have been seen crossing the skies by both pilots and passengers, in one of the busiest air corridors in the world! The source has been identified as both Iran to Israel missiles, targeting each other.

This has led to concerns by security experts that an airliner could inadvertently be shot out of the sky. One passenger on a flight from Amsterdam to Dubai recently asked if they "were seeing fireworks or something else?"

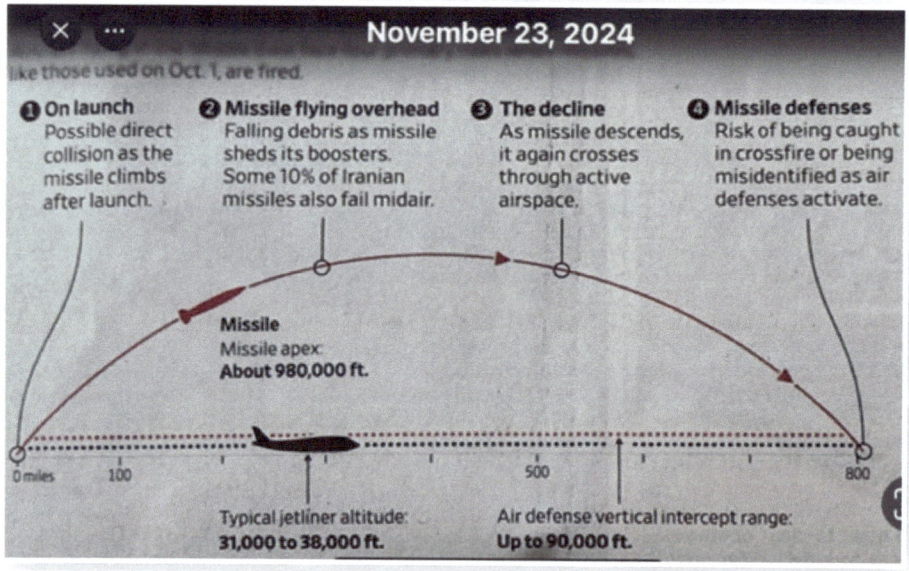

THE A-TEAM

FROM L-R: Auggie and Beth Cipollini, Duane Kinghorn, Tyler Cipollini

The A-Team (Auggie and Beth Cipollini, Duane Kinghorn, Tyler Cipollini), feeling fresh, motivated and ready to kick ass after a 15-hour flight from Miami to Doha, Qatar, **Hamad International Airport**. This is a beautiful, modern airport! We had a short 1-hour layover, then we were off on the next leg of our trip, a 5-hour flight to Kathmandu, Nepal.

"

Wowzaa! Super excited to see you on this trip!! Safe travels.

-NANCY M.

Arriving early in the morning at Tribhuvan International Airport, Kathmandu, Nepal. Greeted by Bhim Panta, owner of Magnificent Himalayan Treks.

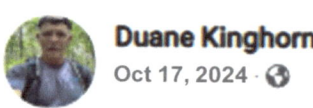

Duane Kinghorn
Oct 17, 2024 · 🌐

Namaste from Nepal, the journey begins to Mount Everest Base Camp! Thank you to everyone that is interested in following our adventure! Many of you have asked how you can follow our team along the way, so the least I can do is take a few minutes each day to share a brief post via Facebook 😎, as long as we can keep a signal.

On Monday, October 14, I left NJ, flying into Ft Lauderdale to meet up with our team, three of the very best, Beth Cipollini, Auggie and Tyler Anne!! No apprehension by this group, we are excited, ready to go and will give it our best shot!!

On Tuesday, October 15 we traveled to Doha, Qatar (15-hour flight), and caught our next flight (into Kathmandu, Nepal (5 hours). We will be in Kathmandu for approx. one day and then will travel to Lukla tomorrow via helicopter, where we will start our 12-day trek to Mt Everest and back 😎!

Thanks again to my NJ Sherpa Eileen for getting me prepared, Ellen my motivational coach 😎and all of you that think I'm out of my mind 😂!! Hope you enjoy coming along with us on our little excursion 🧗‍♂️ 😎!

👍❤️ 105   23 Comments   4 Shares

👍 Like   💬 Comment   ➤ Share

FACEBOOK POST
Duane Kinghorn, Oct. 17, 2024

Magnificent Himalayan Treks (MHT) was the perfect trekking organization for us! From the pre-planning, to the time we departed from the US, to when we landed in Kathmandu, MHT's was with us! That included picking us up and driving us to all destinations, ensuring we were always prepared and on time. We enjoyed the very best hospitality and service from Bhim Panta, owner and operator and his entire team. Bhim sets an amazing example and everyone on the team couldn't have been more friendly and accommodating, answering all our questions and ensuring we always got what we needed and were satisfied! Bhim and his team were always available, extremely helpful throughout the trek, the hospitality was spectacular, couldn't have asked for anything better!

Our guides Ishwor and Sanket (Sanke) were with us every step of the way, they were an amazing resource, very knowledgeable and friendly!

They provided us with assistance in anything we needed, including making important adjustments along the way, always focused on our safety first, while ensuring the best experience.

We were also provided with two porters (Sandesh and Sabin) that carried the bulk of our gear, providing us with an enjoyable experience and allowing us to concentrate on the goal ahead, reaching Mount Everest Base Camp safely and on time.

We can't thank MHT enough for the wonderful experience they provided! The friendships that were established during our trip will always be remembered! As the name implies, they were **"Magnificent"** in every way!

MAGNIFICENT HOTEL
Keshar Mahal Marg, Kathmandu 44600, Nepal

Our first full day in Kathmandu was spent touring parts of the city, getting in some sightseeing and shopping later in the day. We were joined by Bhim, Sanke and Manit who were kind enough to show us around the different markets. We had such a positive experience in Kathmandu and much admiration for the Nepalese citizens that we met.

"

Wow, this is awesome and exciting! I can't wait to see the next post! Enjoy and be safe, my friend!

—PHIL W.

"

DK! This is amazing! I can't wait to follow along! Safe travels!

—JAMIE S.

⦿ KATHMANDU

> ❝
> *It is so exciting. Pictures and updates are amazing!*
>
> —DONNA S.

> ❝
> *You are amazing Duane!! How inspiring (and yes, utterly insane!) you are! Safe travels my friend.*
>
> —KRISTEN K.

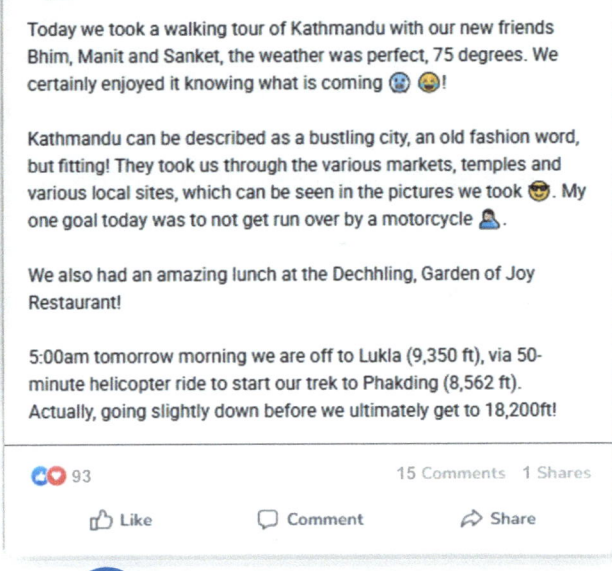

Duane Kinghorn
Oct 17, 2024 · 🌐   ···

Today we took a walking tour of Kathmandu with our new friends Bhim, Manit and Sanket, the weather was perfect, 75 degrees. We certainly enjoyed it knowing what is coming 😱 😄!

Kathmandu can be described as a bustling city, an old fashion word, but fitting! They took us through the various markets, temples and various local sites, which can be seen in the pictures we took 😎. My one goal today was to not get run over by a motorcycle 🏍️.

We also had an amazing lunch at the Dechhling, Garden of Joy Restaurant!

5:00am tomorrow morning we are off to Lukla (9,350 ft), via 50-minute helicopter ride to start our trek to Phakding (8,562 ft). Actually, going slightly down before we ultimately get to 18,200ft!

👍❤️ 93   15 Comments 1 Shares

👍 Like   💬 Comment   ↪ Share

𝗳 FACEBOOK POST

Duane Kinghorn, Oct. 17, 2024, Kathmandu, Nepal

What a fun day touring **Kathmandu**, seeing all the sights, experiencing the local culture first-hand and mentally preparing for the unknown that lies ahead…

 **KATHMANDU**

"

Wow! I am so impressed and excited for you. Looking forward to following the journey.

-DIANE S.

"

Had a great time showing you around! Hope you're ready for what's next!

-MANIT L.

The cost of lunch was 3,340 Rupees, with a tip totaled $30 US dollars.

*3,340 RUPEES = $30 US DOLLARS

Auggie capturing the sites with his *Get-Smart*-like video sunglasses.

This watch kept us on US Eastern Standard time.

📍**DECHENLING GARDEN OF JOY RESTAURANT**
Keshar Mahal Marg, Kathmandu, Nepal 44600

"

Do they have pork roll?

-IRENE R.

This was quite the scene watching motorcycles weaving in and out as pedestrians were walking, shopping and trying to clean the roads!

It was very common seeing telephone poles wrapped in a spaghetti of wires coming from every direction. Not sure how they would ever be able to identify or fix broken wires.

MAGNIFICENT HOTEL
Keshar Mahal Marg, Kathmandu 44600, Nepal

From the comforts of home in Kathmandu, to the real world: Everest Base Camp – *here we come*!

 **WHATSAPP MESSAGE**
From Elieen, October 14, 2024

EVEREST BASE CAMP * TREK ITINERARY

Every Detail You Need for the Journey of a Lifetime

DAY 1 (OCTOBER 18): Fly from Kathmandu to Lukla and Trek to **Phakding village** (2,650m/8,694ft)*

⇒ Flight Time: 50 mins Flight

⇒ Trekking Distance: 9 km/5.6 miles

⇒ Trekking Time: 3-4 Hours

DAY 2: Trek from Phakding to **Namche Bazaar** (3,440m/11,286ft)

⇒ Trekking Distance: 11 km/6.8 miles

⇒ Trekking Time: 6-7 Hours

DAY 3: Acclimatization Day at **Namche Bazaar** (3,880m/12,730ft)

⇒ Trekking Distance: 4.6 km/2.8 miles

⇒ Trekking Time: 3-4 Hours

DAY 4: Trek from Namche Bazaar to **Tengboche** (3,720m/12,205ft)

⇒ Trekking Distance: 13 km/8.12 miles

⇒ Trekking Time: 6-7 Hours

DAY 5: Trek from Tengboche to **Dingboche** (4,410m/14,469ft)

⇒ Trekking Distance: 8.5 km/5.3 miles

⇒ Trekking Time: 5-6 Hours

*Diverted to Surkhe due to poor weather conditions at Lukla. This put us 5 hours south of Phakding.

DAY 6: Acclimatization Day at **Dingboche** (4,800m/15,748ft)

⇒ Trekking Distance: 4.5 km/2.8 miles

⇒ Trekking Time: 4-5 Hours

DAY 7: Trek from Dingboche to **Lobuche** (5,050m/16,568ft)

⇒ Trekking Distance: 9 km/ 5.6 miles

⇒ Trekking Time: 4-5 Hours

DAY 8: Trek from Lobuche to **Gorak Shep** (5,164m/16,942ft), crossing Khumbu Glacier and stay at Gorak Shep

⇒ Trekking Distance: 12 km/7.4 miles

⇒ Trekking Time: 7 Hours

DAY 9: Trek from Gorak Shep to our final destination, ***EVEREST BASE CAMP** (5,364m/17,598ft) and back to Gorak Shep

DAY 10 (OCTOBER 27): Fly from Gorak Shep to Lukla (15 minutes), to Kathmandu (50 minutes)

The first few days of trekking in the Himalayan forest, are in warmer and slightly more moderate temperatures. The second half of the trek takes you into colder and often freezing conditions. On Base Camp itself, temperatures can vary from 1 to -15 degrees, on average. We experienced below freezing temperatures primarily at night.

WHATSAPP MESSAGE

Family Group Chat, October 15, 2024

TENZING-HILLARY AIRPORT
Heliport, Kathmandu

Once we got the green light it was time to go, we quickly got our gear and made our way to the transport vehicle. About 10 of us squished in and off we went to the heliport. The transport vehicle was a safari-like truck, with all the windows open and music playing, which sounded like the same verse playing over and over!

Little did we know that the heliport was on the other side of the airport and would take us almost 30 minutes to get there, while driving over some bumpy, unpaved roads. Although we didn't know, our driver was only taking us to another waiting area, which was very suspect – I will describe that situation in more detail on the next page.

W e left the Magnificent Hotel at 5:30am to catch a 50-minute helicopter flight to Lukla airport, where we waited approx. 5 hours. Once we were given the word it was time to go, we needed to quickly get on our transport vehicle to the heliport, little did we know that was going to be a 30-minute ride around the airport, on dirty roads under construction.

Additionally, we were taken to a holding location close to the heliport on the outskirts of Kathmandu Airport. The holding station consisted of a group of old shipping containers, randomly thrown together, in a somewhat deserted off the road location. A group of 10 of us were escorted, single file, down a path in between the shipping containers to the rear area, where there were a few ripped up couches and chairs that had been exposed to the elements.

*A SUSPECT SITUATION…

It felt like the poor Americans were being walked to our deaths, between these dilapidated shipping containers, where we would be kidnapped for ransom, executed or both!

This is where we waited for over an hour before our helicopter pilot walked across this rugged field between the holding area and the heliport, to brief us on the status of our flight delay to Lukla. While at the same time it was a warm sunny day, around 80 degrees.

Finally, we were given the green light by our pilot that it was "go time" once again and we quickly got our gear and followed our pilot (single file), across this overgrown, desert like field to the heliport.

After arriving at the heliport, we continued to wait for instructions and air traffic controller details. Our pilot, who was South African, became more and more frustrated as time went by. He said this is typical of Kathmandu air traffic control, that would usually not give departure timelines. More sit and wait, not realizing what lies ahead once we got in the air and to our destination, Lukla.

During the long waiting periods, we found spots behind airport transport equipment and fueling carts to go to the bathroom, never knowing who could see what from all directions. This was especially challenging for Beth and Tyler that had to walk through high grasses and weeds over their heads to get to a random, rundown building next to the heliport. Again, what felt like another scene out of a murder mystery thriller…LOL!

*IT'S "GO TIME…"

We got the word it's **"Go Time"** and we were 3-4 in line for departure, anxiety kicking in and heart pounding, we grabbed our gear and got prepared to step onto the helicopter.

Although we were told it was a go, we waited another 30+ minutes, but this time we were fairly confident it was the real thing. The helicopter engines around us were started and they were taking off every 10 minutes.

Luckily, weather conditions were starting to improve for our trek. If it was 2 weeks earlier our trip would have been delayed or canceled. We picked the perfect window thanks to Beth's research and arrangement preparation!

As we lifted into the air there was buzzing excitement, knowing that in less than an hour we'd be stepping into the heart of the Himalayas, about to trace the footsteps of climbers and adventurers who had dreamed of the same path. The helicopter itself felt like a gateway—lifting you out of the city's chaos and carrying you toward the thin mountain air.

At the same time, there was nervous energy—a mix of awe and uncertainty. Would the altitude be kind? Would the legs hold up over the long days of trekking? You could almost feel your heartbeat quicken as you thought of the suspension bridges, the colorful prayer flags fluttering in the wind, and that first glimpse of Everest itself.

There was also a quiet sense of gratitude and wonder—to be in a place so far removed from daily routine, about to live out a dream that few people ever get the chance to attempt. This wasn't just an ordinary trip; it was the beginning of a pilgrimage to the world's rooftop.

FROM L-R: Auggie Cipollini, Tyler Cipollini, Beth Cipollini and Duane Kinghorn

*LET THE FUN BEGIN...

No fear in this group!!

...Sanke is chill, might have taken a Gummy

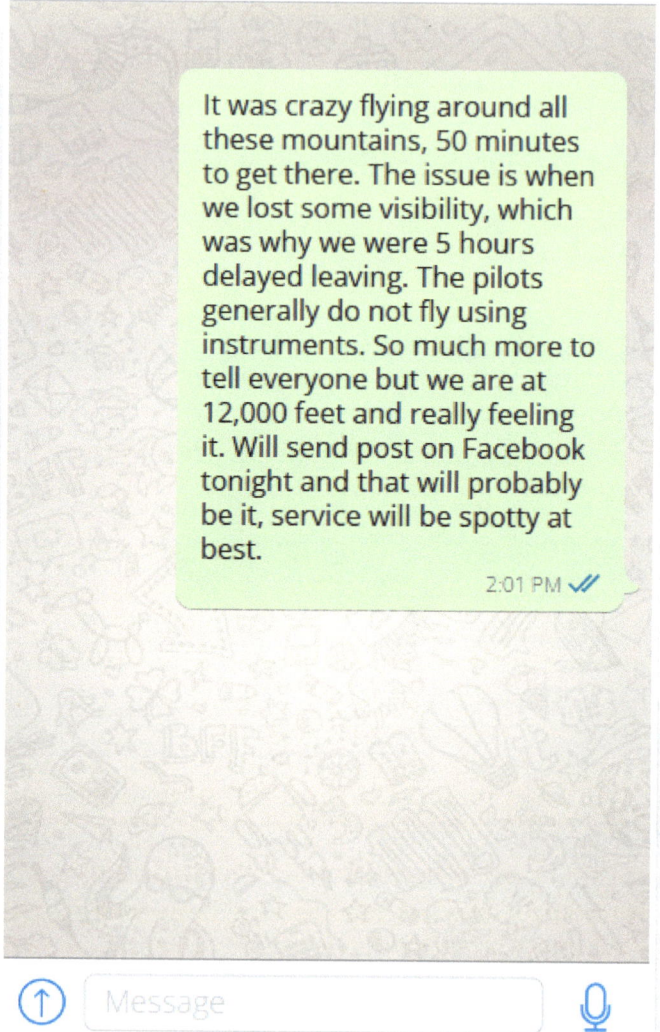

> It was crazy flying around all these mountains, 50 minutes to get there. The issue is when we lost some visibility, which was why we were 5 hours delayed leaving. The pilots generally do not fly using instruments. So much more to tell everyone but we are at 12,000 feet and really feeling it. Will send post on Facebook tonight and that will probably be it, service will be spotty at best.
>
> 2:01 PM ✓✓

 WHATSAPP MESSAGE

Duane Kinghorn, October 15, 2024

Here are the views from the helicopter as we left Kathmandu. Quickly the weather started to change as we traveled through clouds and fog.

Auggie was trying to have a conversation with the pilot, as I was pointing to approaching mountains in front of us. Since the pilot said they mostly fly visually, I was thinking it was probably best that he focused on the task at hand!

Lukla is the first of the villages that you visit in the region when you fly from Kathmandu. As most of the Everest trekkers fly to Lukla, it is also known as the gateway to Everest. With a small airport and beautiful surroundings, Lukla is one of the major villages in the region. Most of the trekking adventures in the Everest region begin and finish in this village. As soon as you land at Lukla, they say you can feel the excitement building. The trail leading you to the base camp stretches towards the higher elevation of mountains from Lukla. However, we only went through Lukla on our return to Kathmandu from base camp. During our initial flight on day 1, we were delayed leaving Kathmandu by approx. 5 hours and during the flight we were diverted to a ridge known as Surkhe Khola, due to heavy fog conditions at Lukla, closing the airport. Surkhe was significantly south of Lukla, adding distance and time to get to our first destination, Phakding.

As we approached Surkhe coming out of the fog, we could see the ridge where we were going to land – a narrow strip of land in front of a small teahouse that was set slightly back on a small hill. As the pilot approached the ridge, he took a sharp left turn and muttered "OMG this is chaos," describing the scene where we were landing. He landed the helicopter on the edge of the cliff, with the tail partially hanging over the cliff...at that point it was time to get out quickly!!

You could see approx. 150 trekkers sitting on the hill anxiously waiting their turn to catch a helicopter out. These were people that were stuck due to poor weather conditions, consisting of heavy rains and blizzard conditions encountered near base camp a week earlier.

📍 LUKLA: THE GATEWAY TO EVEREST
One of the major villages of the region

Lukla is the gateway for all treks in the Khumbu region, including Everest Base Camp. Nestled in the mountains at 2,855m (9,366ft). The majority of people arrive in Lukla by air, landing at the small runway or helicopter pad at Tenzing-Hillary Airport (LUA), considered one of the most dangerous airports in the world! If you prefer not to fly, it's possible to get to Lukla overland in 3+ days, by taking a bus/jeep then trekking on foot…this was an option if we got stuck due to bad weather, but was not optimal.

Flights to Lukla operate year-round from Kathmandu, although cancellations and delays are common as flights can only run in favorable weather conditions. The flight time is approx. 50 minutes from Kathmandu. The Lukla runway is just 527m (1,729ft) long and is sloped at an 11.7% gradient, making taking off and landing challenging for pilots and a little daunting for passengers. Flights usually only operate in the morning, when the skies are clearer and there is less wind.

SOURCE: www.GOINGTHEWHOLEHOGG.com

> **"**
> *Be Safe DK*
> -ALEX K.

> **"**
> *You got this DK!!!*
> -RYAN N.

> **"**
> *Go DK and team!*
> -BILLY F.

Once we got off the helicopter and surveyed the lay of the land, we went into the small teahouse for something to eat. Somehow our order was lost and by the time we realized there was an issue, they were out of chow mein, but we rallied through it and kept on smiling. We were very hungry at this point and would take whatever they had, still having a 5-hour hike ahead of us, with nightfall less than 3 hours away. This put us over 3 hours hiking in the dark, completely out of our element!

> **"**
> *Let's Go Duane! This is incredible!!*
> -KYLE B.

> **"**
> *Hey Buddy! You got this!*
> -JOHN Z.

> **"**
> *Go Duane and Team!!*
> *Stay safe!!*
> -JULIE P.

> **"**
> *Awesome Duane. Stay safe!!*
> -SCOTT M.

Our guide (Ishwor) was also stuck 2 days ahead of us, due to the poor weather conditions experienced at base camp the prior week. Luckily, we were able to have an inexperienced, 20-year-old companion named Sanke (far right in the group picture) to guide the way. Seriously, he was our lifeline in so many ways! He was even labeled my fourth son early in the adventure and of course the inexperienced hiker in the bunch (me) jumped right on that! Sanke knew his way, took care of all stops, meals, kept us safe from animals, etc., but most importantly he was a genuinely nice person and fun to be around!! Since the trip was not starting out as planned, you could see where this was going – survival of the fittest!

> "
> *The pessimist sees difficulty in every opportunity. The optimist sees the opportunity in every difficulty.*
> -WINSTON CHURCHILL

Once we landed, ate and started our trek, it was already late in the day and we were all tired. Five minutes into a steep climb up the first mountain, along a narrow section where we were walking in single file, I slipped and "leaned" into the side of the mountain. The team looked back and saw me on my side thinking I was joking, I wasn't, literally stuck with a full pack and needed help getting back up! It wasn't until we got to the Phakding village later that night that I realized I cut my left elbow, probably on a sharp rock during my lean. Although I didn't feel anything there was blood dripping down my elbow. Looking back, I can say that was my only slip, or preferably the team all agreed it was more of a "lean", during our entire trek. Glad to get that over with early in the trek (first 5 minutes).

Later in the journey I did step in Yak dung, but that was something we all experienced at least once. I guess you could call it a right of passage, which I was so close to avoiding that fate. At the higher elevations we figured out that using the snow banks to kick and clean our shoes, was the best method!

There are many beautiful villages along the EBC trek, they are referred to as Sherpa villages. The Sherpa communities are famous mountain climbing tribes who make it possible for people to experience mountaineering in the Everest region, safely, but also bring the knowledge of the region to life. The cultural and lifestyle experience of the region makes the adventure even more enjoyable and rewarding.

Each village has their own unique qualities and attributes as you make your way to your end goal of Everest Base Camp. This includes teahouses with electric, western style bathrooms and a heated blanket on the lower-level villages, to no electric, no heat, no running water, no western toilet, etc., as you move closer to base camp. Interesting enough, this is where you need those conveniences of everyday life the most – when the elements and extreme weather conditions of wind and cold are the worst! Unfortunately, they did not exist at these higher elevations and during some periods of the year, require residents of these communities to actually relocate to lower levels of the region.

SHERPA VILLAGES
Nepal's Everest region

CHAPTER FOUR

*PHAKDING TREK (DAY 1)

Phakding was our first stop, which was delayed by 5 hours due to poor weather conditions, requiring us to hike over 2 hours in the dark, arriving at 8:30 at night.

Phakding is normally the first overnight stop in the region while trekking to Everest. It is a beautiful village on the bank of the Dudh Koshi River. The other village we went through the next day was Monjo, the main entry point to the Sagarmatha National Park. It is also a popular place to stay overnight while returning back from base camp.

📍**PHAKDING**
Small village in the Khumbu region, Nepal

> "
This is a once in a lifetime experience but at the same time scary. They have this and what an accomplishment this will be. I've been following his adventure and all I can say is WOW! Good thoughts and prayers for a safe trip.

-DENISE M.

⦿PHAKDING

> "
We miss you already...So impressed you're doing this! Be safe and keep us all posted!

-MARYANN T.

*FEAR +
HIGH ALTITUDES

This was our first **suspension bridge** and the team wanted to make sure they captured my every step, from every angle, what a team 😀! As we moved into higher altitudes you could hear your breathing accelerate. This was further elevated for me as I crossed the suspension bridges...fear and high altitude: a bad mix!

"

I would have already turned around. Happy Adventures!

-JO K.

So amazing. Thank you for sharing. I have read books about Everest but it is great to follow along with your journey and watch it unfold!

-VIRGINIA M.

Good luck Duane! Have fun on your crazy adventure. I will stay here and take different shots than the ones you needed for your trip😃.

-ELLIOT L.

*STEEP + ROCKY MOUNTAIN CLIMBS

In addition to our two guides, Sanke and Ishwor, we were assisted by our porters, **Sandesh and Sabin** (picture to the left), who carried two bags each…exceeding 100lbs. So impressive how they managed to do this with ease, up and down steep, rocky mountains over a 9-day period – always with a smile! We couldn't have been more appreciative!

FROM L-R: Sandesh and Sabin

*FOGGY WEATHER CONDITIONS

With the late start of trekking day 1, we experienced mostly mild, cloudy, humid, and foggy weather conditions.

The beginning of suspension bridge hell, first 3 of 8 that we crossed. Tyler and Beth were very amused, while Auggie and I just took it in stride!!

*SUSPENSION BRIDGE HELL

*BREATHTAKING LANDSCAPES

The landscapes everywhere you looked were out of this world; simply amazing!!

*WILDFLOWERS + GARDENS

Combination of wildflowers and village cultivated gardens were seen along the trek!

*RAGING RIVERS

You could see how the raging rivers were changing the landscape, almost real time – not unusual to see landslides throughout our trek.

CHAPTER FIVE
*NAMCHE BAZAAR TREK AND ACCLIMATIZATION –
"THE SHERPA CAPITAL OF EVEREST" (DAYS 2 & 3)

Namche Bazaar is more than just a village. It is the major financial hub in the Everest region. Situated on a beautiful mountain slope at an elevation of 3,440 meters (11,286ft) above sea level. Namche Bazaar can be the true capital town of the region, with the facilities that you would expect in a more modern town. Namche gives a sense of being in a small urban city in the high altitudes of the mountains.

It is not only an overnight stop, but also the first acclimatization point for trekkers, where you hike to the nearest landmark called Syangboche. People hiking to Everest Base Camp spend two nights here on their way up, including us. It is one of the more happening and attractive villages, with 3 bars, restaurants, and shopping in the Everest Base Camp Trek.

NAMCHE BAZAAR
Solukhumbu District of Koshi Province, Nepal

Sagarmatha **National Park**, Nepal is the gateway to Everest Base Camp. Sanke, our guide, waited in line for over an hour with our Visas, to obtain visitor passes, at a cost of 3,000 Nepalese Rupee's. This was a good opportunity to take a needed rest!

⦿ SAGARMATHA NATIONAL PARK
Gateway to Everest Base Camp

*ALL THE COMFORTS OF HOME...

NAMCHE BAZAAR TREK AND ACCLIMATIZATION (DAYS 2 & 3)

49

⟟ THE TREK TO MOUNT EVEREST

Seeing the Dream. Living the Dream.

*THE WORLD'S TALLEST MOUNTAIN

Trekking to the Everest Base Camp and seeing the world's tallest mountain up close is the dream of avid trekkers from all around the world. There is an awesome sense of accomplishment that comes with trekking through an area considered to be one of the toughest for climbing.

Surprisingly, although we were walking in high altitude regions that significantly increased from the start to reaching EBC, we spent a fair amount of time going down steep, rocky inclines.

<big>L</big>ooks like I'm feeling a little cocky on this mini suspension bridge after I crossed a few of the bigger ones earlier in the day!

Duane Kinghorn
Oct 19, 2024 · 🌐

We flew from Kathmandu to Surkhe yesterday, a small town a few hours away from Lukla, as the airport remained closed due to foggy conditions. The helicopter flight was delayed by about 6 hours diverting our flight to Surkhe.

It was an early start yesterday, departed for the airport at 5:00am. I should have videotaped the ride to the airport, there are no traffic signs, lights or street names, will do it when we come back, what an experience 😎! It was a free for all, but our driver was amazing, dodging cars, dogs, motorcycles and people, they would have no issues with our NJ roundabouts 😅.

They have been experiencing some of the worst weather conditions in years. Which delayed our helicopter departure by 6 hours, diverting us to Surkhe. When the pilot landed on the edge of a cliff 🧗, you could hear him say "this is chaos", trying to also fly out all those that got stranded due to last week's bad weather. That 50-minute helicopter ride was like nothing we have ever experienced and somewhat scary as we flied around the mountains in foggy conditions.

So, we had lunch at Surkhe, watching all the action and then hiked almost 5 hours to Phakding, over 2 hours in the dark up the steep mountain, arriving around 8:30🧗.

Today we hiked to Namche, about 8 miles almost all of it uphill, see some great pictures we took. We are all starting to feel the attitude, currently at 12k feet and are very tired at night. This will be the last post until we complete the trip, but will try to continue to post pictures as long as we have coverage. Thanks for all the notes of encouragement! Will send pictures tomorrow after I recharge my batteries.

👍❤️ 142   25 Comments 9 Shares

👍 Like   💬 Comment   ➤ Share

 **FACEBOOK POST**
Duane Kinghorn, Oct. 19, 2024

Early in our trek, Beth received a call with no message. The name that came up on the caller ID was Michael Walsh. What made this significant, this was the name of Beth's brother who passed away over 50 years ago.

After a rough start on the first day of our trek, this clearly felt like a sign that Michael and others were walking with us on our adventure! A similar situation occurred when Beth and Auggie were in Kilimanjaro. A gentleman with the name Duane, replaced me on the trek. He also went by the name Mike and looked like Uncle Frank, Beth's father who recently had passed away. Just like then, we were feeling blessed!

*MONJO ELEVATION 2855M

"

Eileen, I guess you will think twice when Duane suggests you and him go for a walk...lol

-JOANNE R.

*PROMOTING GREAT BRANDS ALONG THE WAY

A little shameless promotion…representing the **Citigroup Premier Credit Card, ProCare Rehabilitation** and the **Orbit of Love organization**. I was hedging my bets on day 2 of our trip by taking these pictures, just in case we didn't make EBC…but never a doubt!

CITIGROUP   PROCARE   ORBIT OF LOVE

> **"**
> *Awesome pictures! What an incredible journey is about to take place. Sending positivity, prayers, Love!*
>
> –ELAINE M.

Eileen Kinghorn
Oct 19, 2024 · 🌐

Where in the world are Duane Kinghorn, Tyler Anne, Auggie and Beth Cipollini? This crew is in Nepal, attempting the trek of a lifetime to Mt. Everest Base Camp. Duane is an avid walker and runner, but you will usually find him on the golf course since he retired. When Beth invited him to join this adventure, he jumped at the challenge. After 19 hours of flights, they arrived in Kathmandu.

The weather conditions have been terrible the last few weeks, so they switched from a small plane ride to a helicopter to get to their starting point in Lukla. After a 6-hour fog delay, they took a harrowing, 50-minute helicopter ride to Surkhe. Then they hiked 5 hours, 2 in the dark, up the mountain to Phakding.

Yesterday they hiked 8 miles to Namche. They are at 12,000 feet and will hike to the base camp at 18,000. Take a close look at the pictures and you will see the suspension bridges they are crossing. Absolutely frightening and breathtaking at the same time. Sending all our positive energy and prayers for their safety during the trip. ⚠️

❤️👍 109   20 Comments   2 Shares

👍 Like   💬 Comment   ↗ Share

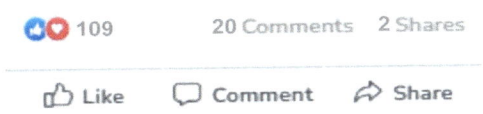

f FACEBOOK POST
Eileen Kinghorn, Oct. 19, 2024

The Hillary Bridge is the tallest suspension bridge in Nepal at 443ft high and 197ft in length…a beast!

📍**THE HILLARY BRIDGE**
Tallest Suspension Bridge, Nepal

Reaching Namche felt like stepping into the beating heart of the Everest region. After days of trekking through quiet valleys and across dizzying suspension bridges strung with prayer flags, the village revealed itself like a hidden amphitheater carved into the mountainside. The air was thinner here, but the energy of the place was alive and vibrant. The colorful arc of houses and shops, all stacked in terraces against the steep slope, seemed to cling impossibly to the hillside. It was a crossroads of cultures; the starting point for expeditions, the marketplace for trading, and the resting place where climbers paused before venturing higher.

> **"**
> *You rock my friend. Happy to see you living life to the fullest. What a great journey you are on. Enjoy!*
>
> **-CARLOS O.**

*GOLF UPDATES FROM ACROSS THE GLOBE

Across the globe and I was still getting golf updates!

"6 straight pars at Charleston North. Miss You!"

-MATT K.

"...and now for the real news, LOL"

-JOANNE R. (reply)

"Keep on keeping on! Protein bars and water, be careful coach! Lefty's are up 2 at the turn by the way."

-JOHN (BEANS) M.

"Keep going! I think you can drive the par 5s at 12K ft."

-MIKE M.

"Let me know if you find one of Alex Kondas' drives in the woods out there."

-TOM C.

Duane Kinghorn
Oct 20, 2024 · 🌐

Here are some pictures from our first 2 days hiking. We are having an amazing but challenging time, currently at 12k, all our oxygen levels and heart rates are good.

Today we are spending most of the time in Namche, taking a few hour hike to Hotel Everest View, where we get the first glimpse of Mount Everest 😎!!

For my golf buddies that played yesterday, I'm tracking you on the Grint, so there is no hiding even at 12k feet 😄!

👍❤️ 97   15 Comments 5 Shares

👍 Like   💬 Comment   ↪ Share

FACEBOOK POST
Duane Kinghorn, Oct. 20, 2024

NAMCHE BAZAAR TREK AND ACCLIMATIZATION (DAYS 2 & 3)

*SNEAKY PHOTOGRAPHY
ON THE BRIDGE

Tyler loved teasing me on the suspension bridges (for good reason) and sneaking in some photography to capture the moments!

See that sinister smile!

*THE FIRST VIEW

This was our first view of Mount Everest.

Eileen Kinghorn
Oct 20, 2024 · 🌐

The crew is getting closer to the top of the world! They are still 4 days away from Mt. Everest Base Camp, but were able to see 8 of the 10 highest peaks today. They are in awe of their surroundings. Duane said it's just amazing, unbelievable and indescribable! ⛰️

👍❤️ 150   33 Comments 5 Shares

👍 Like   💬 Comment   ➤ Share

f FACEBOOK POST
Eileen Kinghorn, Oct. 20, 2024

*THE MOST ENCHANTING VIEWS

> **"**
> *What an amazing challenge and*
> *adventure!!! Safe travels and God Bless...*
> *the views are spectacular!!!!*
>
> **-LISA H.**

*EXOTIC ANIMALS

The variety of animals in the **Sagarmatha National Park** was incredible. Luckily, we experienced minimal contact with them. The goal was to avoid bears and leopards at all cost!!

 SAGARMATHA NATIONAL PARK

If the accommodations at Namche Bazaar were the norm throughout our trek, this was going to be a piece of cake. I think Beth knew better of what's to come (see top right)😃! Also, Namche is where we met our guide Ishwor for the first time.

Can it really be this good?

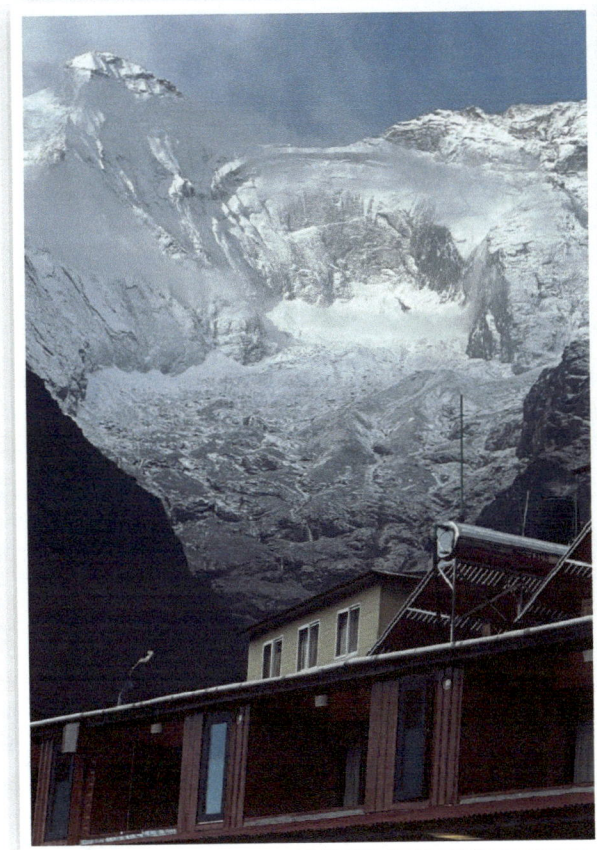

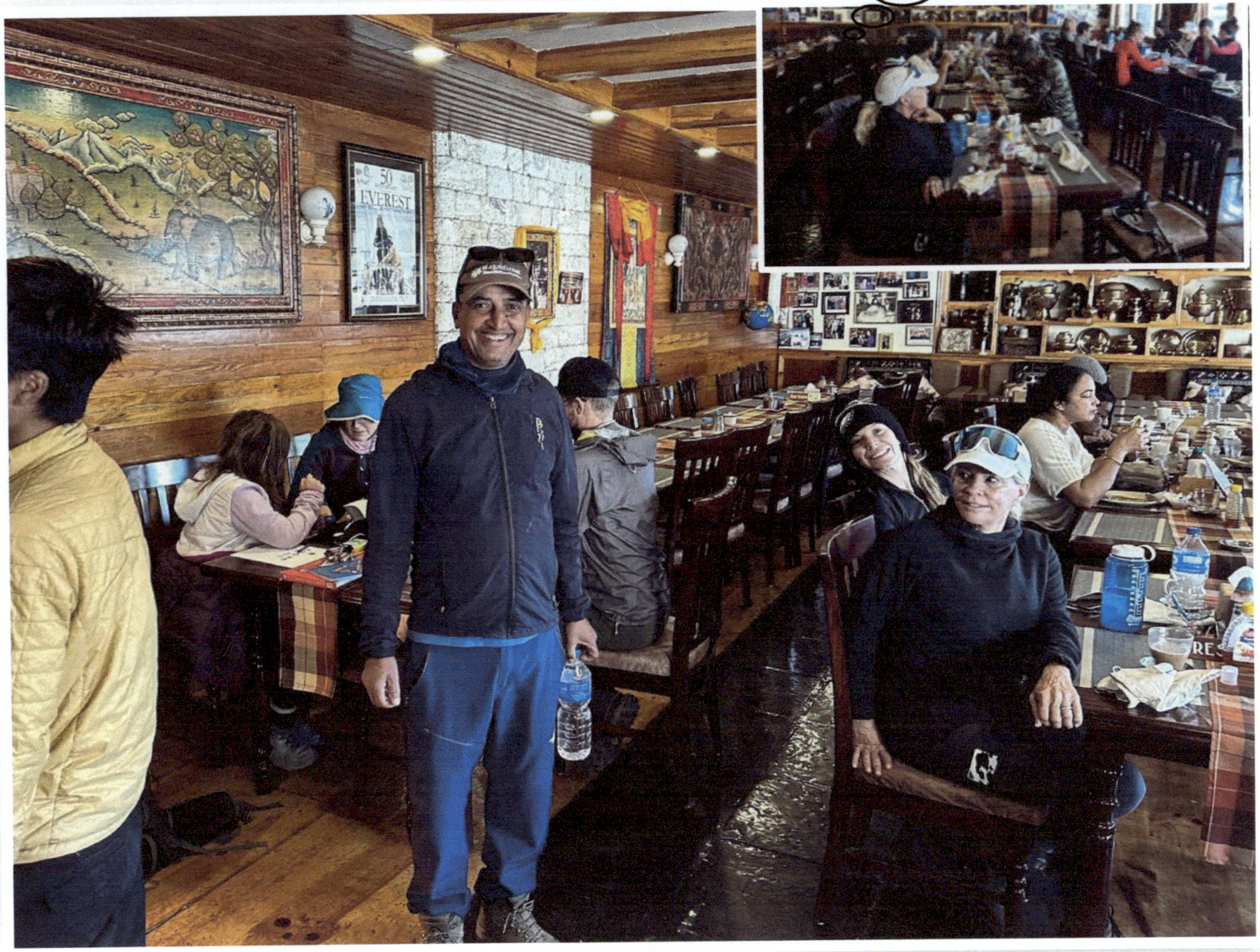

NAMCHE BAZAAR ACCOMMODATIONS

It wasn't unusual to hear dogs barking at night. But one night, a little after 2:00am, many dogs started barking at the same time for a good 30 minutes. It was clear that an animal, possibly a leopard or bear, came down from the mountain and created a lot of anxiety for the dogs!! You could eventually hear the barking become more and more faint, as they were chasing something out of the village.

> "
> *What everyone else said, madness, what the heck! See you in base camp South.*
>
> -MIKE L.

> **"**
> *Hey Buddy, we're all proud of you guys! Don't step in that Yak shit!*
>
> **-JOHN Z.**

Namche was more than just a stopover - it's the cultural and emotional gateway to Everest. This is where you can meet fellow trekkers, share stories with Sherpas and get much needed rest for the challenges to come! Where golden light spills over the terraced roofs, the distant peaks glowing in the afternoon sun and the hum of the village quieting as the night falls.

Our acclimatization day was as memorable as the trek itself. The climb up to the **Everest View Hotel** was steep and demanding, but the reward was unforgettable - our first panoramic glimpse of Everest, Lhotse and Ama Dablam. The hotel offers a 360-degree view of these awe, inspiring peaks! Seeing Everest rise above the surrounding peaks was almost surreal, a moment that stitched together the sharp reality of the mountains standing before us.

> **"**
> *Incredible! I'm getting an education from this trek! Amazing pictures Eileen! Still can't believe it!*
>
> -MARYANN T.

This picture was taken outside the teahouse dining room where we were staying at Namche Bazaar. First time I looked out the window and saw this I thought I was in the middle of a James Bond thriller…all that was missing was *Pussy Galore* or *Beautiful Rachel* (that story I left for later) jumping out of a helicopter 😄! Spectacular, bigger than life view!!

Tyler navigating her way down this steep incline/steps. At the bottom of the hill, you can see a sherpa carrying plastic bottles. The load on his back was so wide, we had to practically move off the path to give him room!

📍 NAMCHE BAZAAR

*SAGARMATHA NEXT PROGRAM

Sagarmatha Next is a cultural center we visited in Sagarmatha National Park, Namche Bazaar. Sagarmatha Next strives to promote sustainable tourism in the Khumbu region of Nepal. The aim is to change the perception around waste and provide support to the local stakeholders of the region, by bringing innovative and sustainable solutions for solid waste management.

Hand of Everest

-BENJAMIN VON WONG,
CLIMATE ACTIVIST

⚲ SAGARMATHA NEXT CULTURAL CENTER
Sagarmatha National Park, Namche Bazaar

*SAGARMATHA NEXT PROGRAM

One creative way to deal with the waste is through a program called **"Carry Me Back."** This is a crowdsourced waste removal system designed to send waste to where it can be recycled by utilizing the movement of locals and tourists to transport items like plastic bottles from the region back to Kathmandu recycling centers.

Even though continuous efforts have been taken by the **Sagarmatha Pollution Control Committee (SPCC)** and various local stakeholders to collect and manage the waste, the challenge is still "what to do with the collected waste?" At present most of it is left behind in numerous pits (+75) that are dug throughout the Khumbu Valley and Sagarmatha National Park, where most of the waste is simply burnt. The lack of infrastructure in the high regions and the difficulty to transport it out of the valley has required creative solutions to manage the waste.

80,000	790KG	200 TONS
VISITORS / YEAR	WASTE PER DAY	WASTE PER YEAR

Thank you for helping keep the hiking trails of Mt. Everest clean.
Your product is entirely made from recycled HDPE bottle caps.

made by moware design

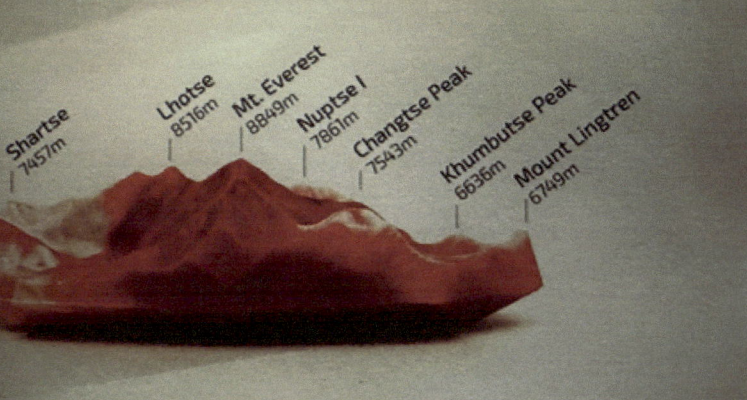

The Himalaya's most iconic peaks

Shartse 7457m · Lhotse 8516m · Mt. Everest 8849m · Nuptse I 7861m · Changtse Peak 7543m · Khumbutse Peak 6636m · Mount Lingtren 6749m

SOURCE: https://www.sagarmathanext.com/

*I made a small donation to support the pollution control efforts, receiving this souvenir of the Himalaya's most iconic peaks made out of bottle caps.

Beth described perfectly what an amazing day we had trekking to Namche Bazaar!!

"

Yesterday was incredible! Walking through small villages meeting beautiful people. We all got a hot shower last night in the beautiful town of Namche Bazaar. What a treat! Those bridges gave us the most beautiful views of rushing water with huge mountains beside. I will never forget this day, Love!

–BETH CIPOLLINI

*MORE SUSPENSION BRIDGE ANTICS

Why not end the Namche Bazar trek with a little more **suspension bridge fun** – at my expense of course!!

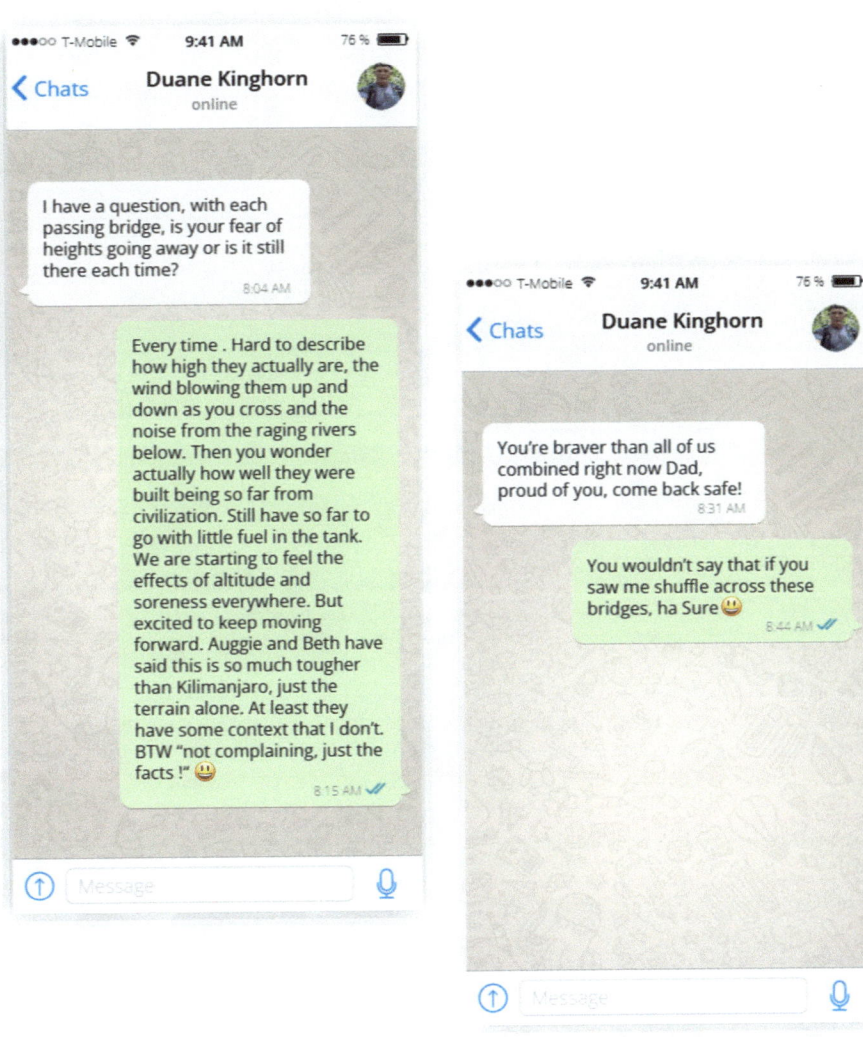

> I have a question, with each passing bridge, is your fear of heights going away or is it still there each time?
> 8:04 AM

> Every time . Hard to describe how high they actually are, the wind blowing them up and down as you cross and the noise from the raging rivers below. Then you wonder actually how well they were built being so far from civilization. Still have so far to go with little fuel in the tank. We are starting to feel the effects of altitude and soreness everywhere. But excited to keep moving forward. Auggie and Beth have said this is so much tougher than Kilimanjaro, just the terrain alone. At least they have some context that I don't. BTW "not complaining, just the facts !" 😄
> 8:15 AM

> You're braver than all of us combined right now Dad, proud of you, come back safe!
> 8:31 AM

> You wouldn't say that if you saw me shuffle across these bridges, ha Sure 😄
> 8:44 AM

WHATSAPP MESSAGES
From Matt, October 20, 2024

CHAPTER SIX
*TENGBOCHE TREK –
CULTURAL CENTER OF THE REGION (DAY 4)

Tengboche is another main village in the region, which is also the major cultural center. In addition to its beautiful location and surroundings, the village also has a **Tengboche Monastery**. The monastery is the cultural center of the Sherpa people living in the region. There are several monasteries in the region, while Tengboche Monastery is the main center of faith for the people. This monastery is known to have been destroyed and rebuilt several times in history and has a major significance in the Buddhist culture.

We spent the night at the village of Tengboche, allowing us to rest and explore the Tengboche Monastery and the village. Pictures below were leaving Namche, heading to the next destination, Tengboche.

TENGBOCHE
Village in Khumbu Pasanglhamu, Nepal

Tengboche Monastery, also known as **Dawa Choling Gompa**, in the Tengboche village in the Khumbu region of eastern Nepal, is a Tibetan Buddhist monastery of the Sherpa community. Situated at 3,867m (12,687 ft), the monastery is the largest gompa in the Khumbu region of Nepal. It was built in 1916 by Lama Gulu with strong links to its mother monastery known as the Rongbuk Monastery in Tibet.

In 1934, it was destroyed by an earthquake and was subsequently rebuilt. In 1989, it was destroyed for a second time by a fire and then rebuilt with the help of volunteers and international assistance.

Tengboche Monastery is located in the Sagarmatha National Park (a UNESCO World Heritage Site of "outstanding universal value"). The monastery attracts large number of tourists for trekking and mountaineering each year.

SOURCE: WIKIPEDIA, The Free Encyclopedia, Tengboche Monastery

 TENBOCHE MONASTERY

*TIBETAN BUDDHIST MONASTERY OF THE SHERPA COMMUNITY

The Tengboche Monastery is constructed with stone masonry. The courtyard and storerooms are large to facilitate the monks' religious activities. The main building has the mandatory Dokhang and prayer hall, where a large statue of **Shakyamuni Buddha** is located. The statue extends to two floors of the monastery and encompasses the first-floor shrine room. We also had an opportunity to observe the daily prayer service.

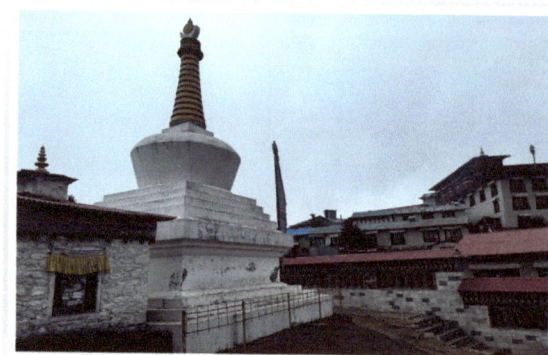

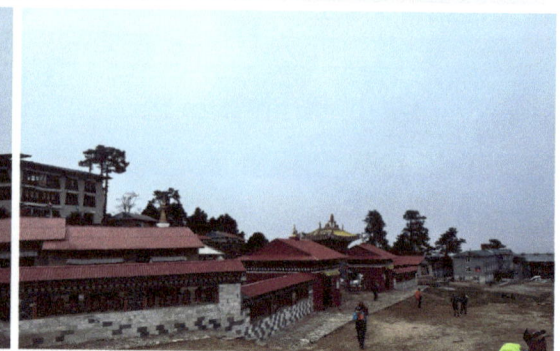

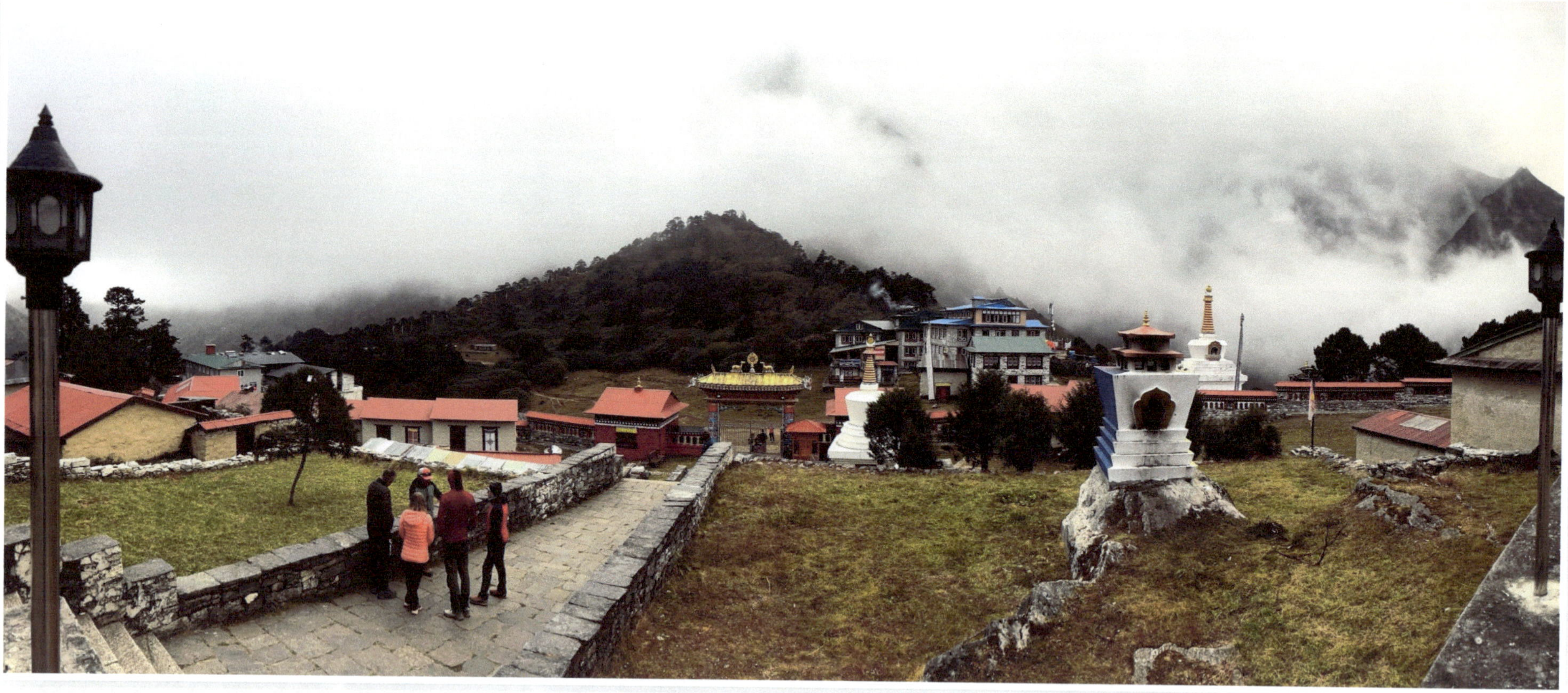

*MORE BREATHTAKING LANDSCAPES

*THE INCREDIBLE SHERPA

The distribution of supplies in the Himalayas are primarily handled by Yaks, porters and helicopters. It was amazing to see this in real time and experience the increasing costs of supplies as we got close to base camp. For instance, a liter bottle of water cost 100 rupees at the first teahouse on our trek and when we got to the last village in our trek, Gorak Shep it increased to 500 rupees!

Yaks doing all of the heavy lifting!

This was completely insane – this sherpa was carrying plastic water bottles on his back *for miles!*

*THE TEAM ANTICS...

The scenery and the views were amazing every day from every angle you looked! Another suspension bridge on the way to Tengboche, not as high as the others, but very bouncy and loud going over the raging river below. This might have been the one where I was set up by the team – they were jumping up and down behind me creating a very uncomfortable situation for me!!

*THE TEAM ANTICS AGAIN...

Found time every day to have some fun, always laughing and joking, even when we were completely spent, probably because we were completely spent!

These wild flowers were growing out of the rocks at the higher elevations, under extreme, cold conditions…incredible!

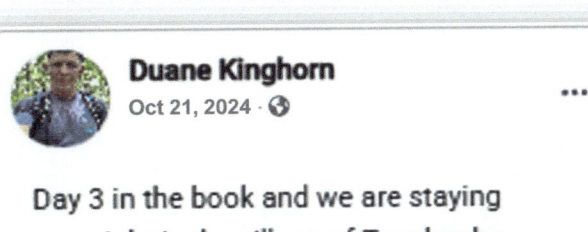

Duane Kinghorn
Oct 21, 2024 · 🌐

Day 3 in the book and we are staying overnight in the village of Tengboche, approx. 12,900 feet. Tomorrow, we hike to Dingboche, 14,300 feet, that will be a great test for us…as my next-door neighbor Maryann said, "this is getting real 😂😎!"

These are some of the pictures I took along our 7 miles today. The team have many more and I'm sure much better than these, that hopefully Eileen will be able to select from the shared album and send more later 😎!

Thanks for all the great notes of encouragement from everyone, it really makes a difference, especially the funny ones! Hope we can keep service as long as possible.

❤️👍 97   15 Comments   2 Shares

👍 Like   💬 Comment   ↪ Share

FACEBOOK POST
Duane Kinghorn, Oct. 21, 2024

"

Omg! Am so in awe of this group of people! Amazing, amazing sights an amazing feat to accomplish. You are right no words to describe!! Be safe everyone stay healthy.

-KAREN M.

*SAFETY AT AMAZING HEIGHTS!

So amazing, Duane… as long as you stay safe!

-PATTY C.

Duane - amazing pictures!"

-DAVE S.

This is one of my favorite pictures, the landscape is incredible, with small houses nestled in the mountain terrain, over shadowed by the massive mountains in the background! On the next page I enlarged a portion of the picture, where you can better see the small village on the hill, that gives greater context to the enormity of these huge mountains!

*LANDSCAPE ZOOMED IN...

"
Congratulations!
Sounds like an
amazing experience!
Those pictures are
unbelievable.

-BETH F.

*DIMINISHING ACCOMMODATIONS

Here are some examples of our accommodations that changed significantly as we progressed closer to base camp. We went from running water, electric outlets, charging station, even an electric blanket one night to no frills!

They look cozy and warm, but it was actually like sleeping on ice, while fully dressed in our sleeping bags!

⦿ SAGARMATHA NATIONAL PARK
The Mount Everest View

This section of **Sagarmatha National Park** provided us with views of Mount Everest for the first time.

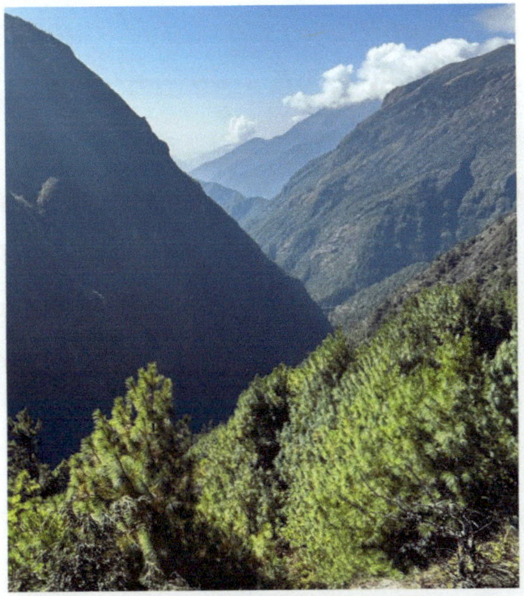

*THE CHORTENS OF NEPAL

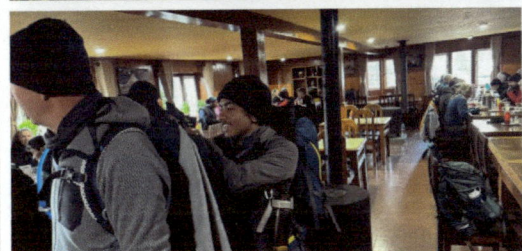

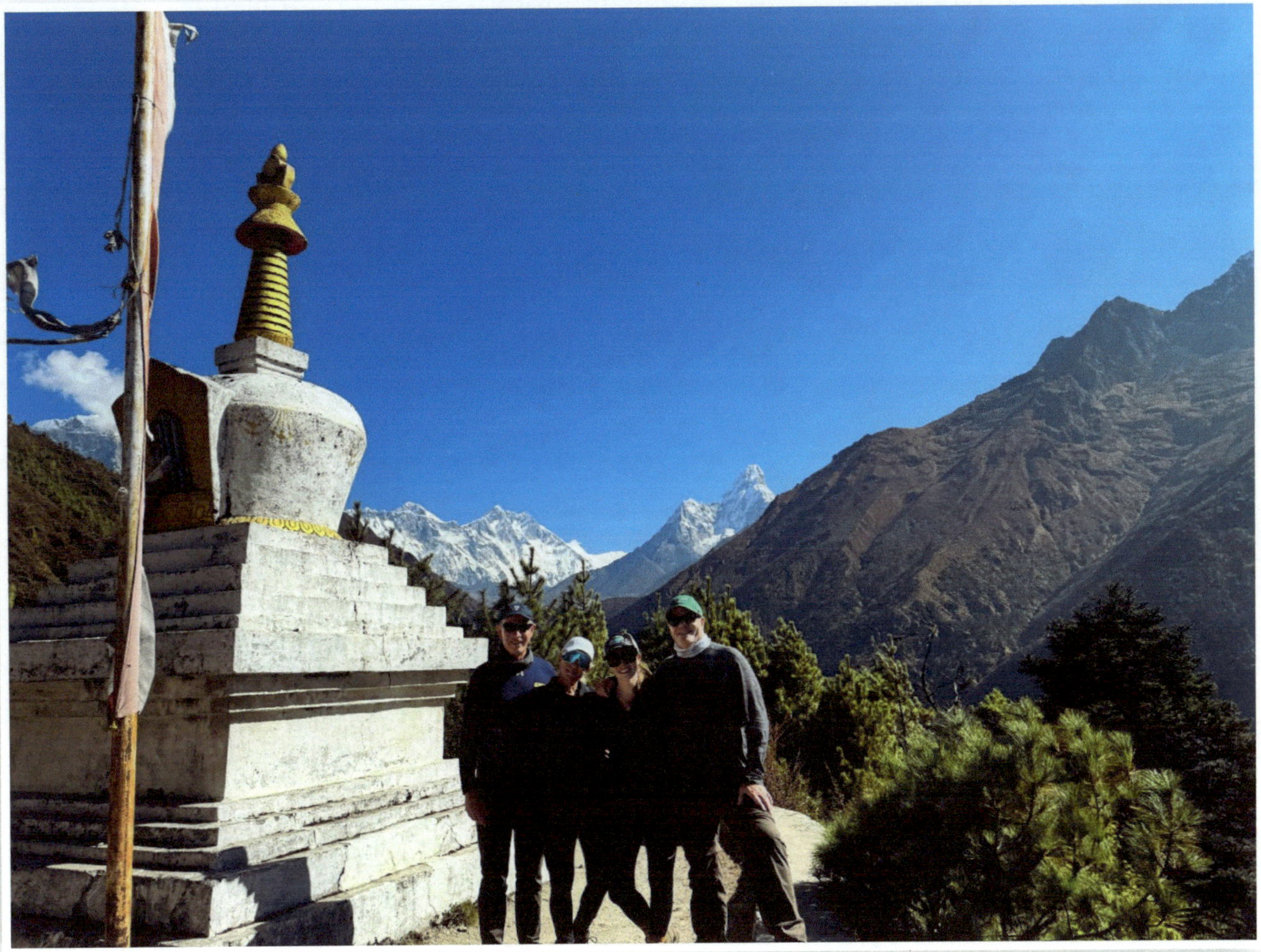

Sanke making some needed adjustments to my pack as we head out for the day, or does he have something else up his sleeve? Not sure based on that smirk.

This was a conversation that my Physical Therapist had with my doctor after I had surgery on November 14, 2024 to repair a torn tendon in right elbow. This was an injury completely unrelated to our trek and scheduled for when I returned. Who needed that arm anyway, as long as my legs were working😀!

> " *Common extensor was completely ruptured off bone and retracted about a centimeter. I've only seen that one other time, crazy! And he climbed to Mount Everest with that, Badass!*
>
> -DR. N.

*TYLER'S AT IT AGAIN...

Whenever I saw that big smile, I knew Tyler was up to something! See her waving her hand over her father's head? Hmmm... what could that be?

> ❝
> *The smiles tell it all. Enjoyment of the experience!*
>
> -PHIL W.

Our friend holding the Famous Parrot!

📍 **TENGBOCHE TREK**

CHAPTER SEVEN

*DINGBOCHE TREK AND ACCLIMATIZATION –

SECOND ACCLIMATIZATION POINT TO EBC (DAYS 5 & 6)

Dingboche is another beautiful village in the region where you get to spend two nights as part of acclimatization. It is a village that is at an elevation of 4,410 meters (14,468ft) above sea level, where you can explore the mountain wilderness. Although it is a small village, the beauty of nature and the mountains it offers is simply incredible.

As part of the critical acclimatization process, we went on a day hike to **Nangkartshang Peak**, another landmark, which is very close to Dingboche. Upon completion of the hike, we returned to the village and spent the night at the Green Tara Guest House.

📍NANGKARTSHANG PEAK
Hiking area in Khumjung, Nepal

Approximately 2 miles west of Dingboche is "Duane Mountain." This was an unnamed location that the team decided to rightly name after this great explorer! There was a landslide recently at the base of the mountain, shown in the pictures below. Tyler accurately described the ruggedness of the mountain in her video!

Landslide on January 26, 2025 just above Pheriche, under Ama Dablam.

📍 **"DUANE MOUNTAIN"**
Two miles west of Dingboche

*DAY 5 TREKKING INTO DINGBOCHE VILLAGE

Long day of hiking as we left Tengboche early in the morning and entered the village of
Dingboche later that day – enjoy the videos capturing us entering the village!

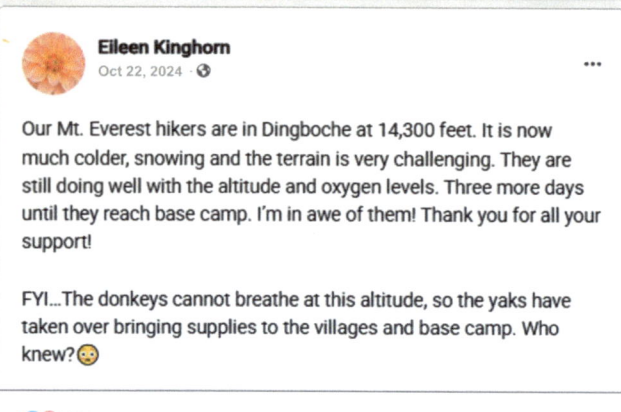

Eileen Kinghorn
Oct 22, 2024 · 🌐

Our Mt. Everest hikers are in Dingboche at 14,300 feet. It is now much colder, snowing and the terrain is very challenging. They are still doing well with the altitude and oxygen levels. Three more days until they reach base camp. I'm in awe of them! Thank you for all your support!

FYI...The donkeys cannot breathe at this altitude, so the yaks have taken over bringing supplies to the villages and base camp. Who knew? 😳

👍❤️ 151   30 Comments 5 Shares

👍 Like   💬 Comment   ↗ Share

FACEBOOK POST
Eileen Kinghorn, Oct. 22, 2024

> "
> *Absolutely awesome, I can't wait for each post!*
>
> -PATTY L.

*GETTING CLOSER TO BASE CAMP...

The closer we got to base camp, the more rock slides we saw in the higher elevations.

Eileen Kinghorn
Oct 23, 2024 · 🌐

The crew had an acclimation day yesterday in Dingboche. Everyone is doing well. They did more hiking, exploring and took in the stunning scenery. Still a few suspension bridges to cross 😳. They plan to reach Everest Base Camp Friday morning (Thursday night our time). ⚠️

👍❤️ 98   15 Comments   2 Shares

👍 Like   💬 Comment   ↗ Share

FACEBOOK POST
Eileen Kinghorn, Oct. 23, 2024

> *You guys are amazing! So happy you are enjoying another adventure, but can't wait for you to get HOME!! Big hugs!!*
>
> —MARY C.

*THE WIDE-RANGING VISTA OF THE HIMALAYAS!

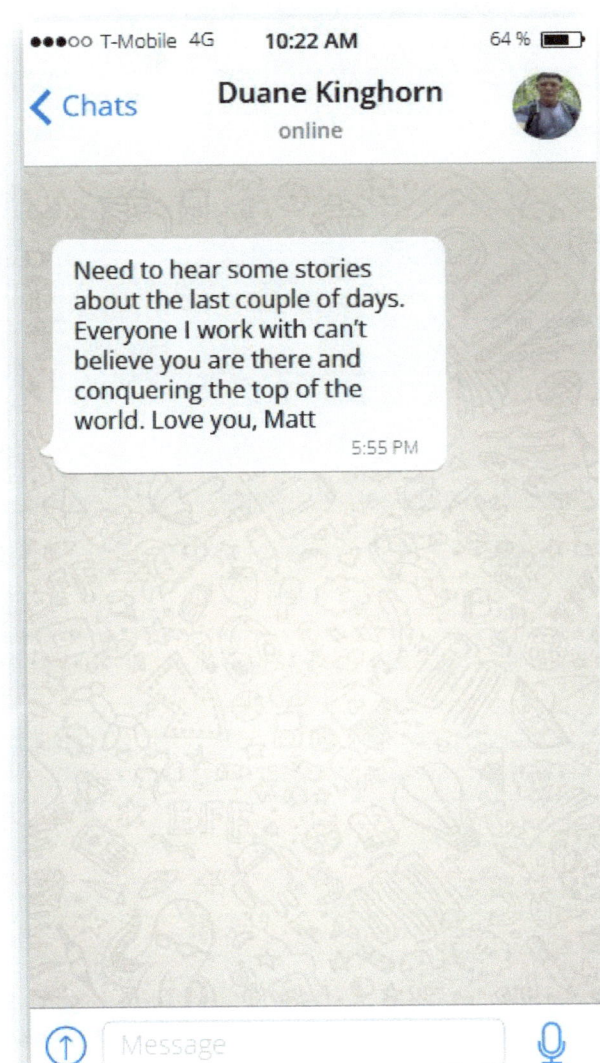

> Need to hear some stories about the last couple of days. Everyone I work with can't believe you are there and conquering the top of the world. Love you, Matt

5:55 PM

Duane Kinghorn — online

> " This is totally amazing Duane…so incredibly awesome…be safe!!! Very proud of you! Congratulations!! Your journey was so inspiring!!!

-JUDY N.

WHATSAPP MESSAGE
From Matt, October 22, 2024

> **You got this - Don't EVER-REST!**
>
> -ADAM R.

> **Your dad needs to give a Jets locker room speech… that's heroic as Fuck.**
>
> -MATT P.

tycip 2h

GUESS WHAT

We're still not there yet...

Tyler and Sanke getting out of the way of the thundering yaks!

Auggie found this beautiful rock, and stopped for a few minutes to take a picture and enjoy the sparkling gems glowing in the bright sunlight – you think altitude sickness was kicking in? We did!

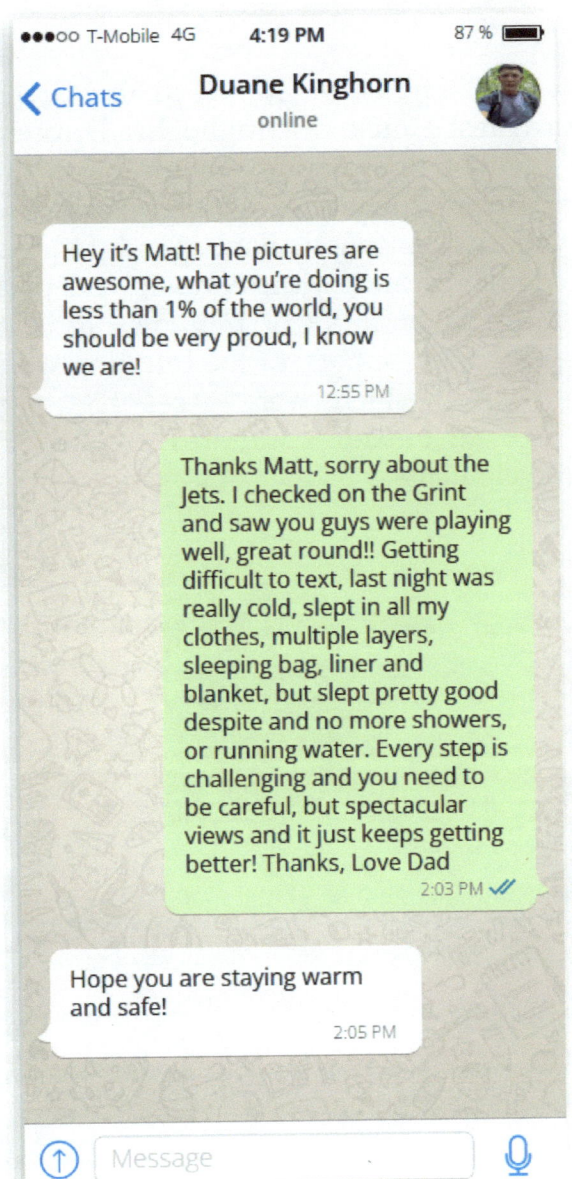

The power of the rivers flowing from the glaciers and melting snow was an incredible site to see and hear! You could see how the landscape was constantly changing as the water flowed through the mountains, carving new designs and views.

Including video of us going over one of the last suspension bridges — and as you can see my confidence level has improved significantly 😀!

Messages shown in screenshot:

Hey it's Matt! The pictures are awesome, what you're doing is less than 1% of the world, you should be very proud, I know we are!
12:55 PM

Thanks Matt, sorry about the Jets. I checked on the Grint and saw you guys were playing well, great round!! Getting difficult to text, last night was really cold, slept in all my clothes, multiple layers, sleeping bag, liner and blanket, but slept pretty good despite and no more showers, or running water. Every step is challenging and you need to be careful, but spectacular views and it just keeps getting better! Thanks, Love Dad
2:03 PM

Hope you are staying warm and safe!
2:05 PM

DINGBOCHE

This is the tea house where I misplaced my Murse, searching and running around in a panic like a crazy person!

For 2 nights we stayed at the **Green Tara Guest House** in **Dingboche**. Through the blanket door in this picture was the common area teahouse where we ate and played backgammon. Sanke and I never played before and by the end we were pros – I think I won 2 out of 15 games, at best. Then toward the back of the building were our rooms, which were accessible only through an outside courtyard exposed to all the elements.

CHAPTER EIGHT

*LOBUCHE TREK (DAY 7)

Lobuche is less of a cultural destination and more of a rural region, overnight stop, where you can get something to eat and rest on your way to EBC.

❝

Beautiful. Amazing all the little villages along the way!

-DAWN K.

📍 LOBUCHE
Mountain in Khumbu Region, Nepal

❝

My Father-in-Law is So Cool! He's currently hiking Mount Everest!

-TAYLOR K.

Love this picture of father and daughter taking a break, as we climbed to the highest mountain in the world!!

 **Eileen Kinghorn**
Oct 24, 2024 · 🌐

···

1 day to go!! Duane wanted to share an update of their adventures the past few days. They are ready to reach Mt. Everest Base Camp tomorrow. IT'S GO TIME! ⛰️

"We had no service the last couple of days, but when we got to Lobuche we had some WiFi service, so I thought I would send this quick post on how we are doing and what's next 😎. This is quite a challenge, that is an understatement 🧗, with all the elements and going straight up on a lot of the climb. However, the sites are amazing and we all agreed it is impossible to describe!! Day 4 we hiked from Tengboche (13,000ft) to Dingboche (14,300ft).

Day 5 was a rest day in Dingboche to acclimate to the altitude. However, not so much 😅, they took us up a 16,000ft mountain and back down, about 3.5 miles straight up hill!

Today (day 6) we hiked to Lobuche (16,300ft).

Tomorrow, we trek to Everest Base Camp 17,600ft, our final destination ❄️, back to Gorek Shep (17,000ft) to spend the night. But if we feel good, we may hike to Kala Pathan viewpoint (18,200ft)🧗, and back to Gorek Shep, where we head back to civilization 😎.

All I really want right now is a pork roll, egg and cheese sandwich, and a Dunkin Ice Coffee 😅!"

Show less

👍❤️ 134   13 Comments 5 Shares

👍 Like   💬 Comment   ↪ Share

 **FACEBOOK POST**
Eileen Kinghorn, Oct. 24, 2024

The landscapes, terrain and views were sensational from every angle you looked. Luckily the breaks required for trekking in high altitude locations gave us the opportunities to frequently take in all of our surroundings!

*SENSATIONAL VIEWS FROM EVERY ANGLE

> **"**
> *What an adventure of a lifetime! Yes, sending prayers and positive vibes to Duane and everyone! Something you can tell the grandkids about! Hang in there Eileen!*
>
> –JEAN P.

*PRAYERS & POSITIVE VIBES INCOMING...

*MOVING INTO HIGHER ELEVATIONS…

Tyler checking in on Mom and Dad as we moved into higher elevations!

The **Famous Parrot** makes another stop in Lobuche!

We learned to move over for these guys…they stopped for NO one!

Great picture and moment capturing mother and daughter enjoying the trip of a lifetime!

*MAKING
MEMORIES OF
A LIFETIME!

THUKLA PASS
Majestic Mountain Pass, Everest Region, Nepal

Thukla Pass: A solemn memorial on the Everest Base Camp Trek, paying homage to the brave climbers who have lost their lives on the slopes of the Himalayan peaks.

Every memorial tells a story, offering a heartfelt salute to those who dared to ascend Everest. Providing trekkers with a moving reminder of the dangers of high-altitude mountaineering and the spirit of those who've attempted it.

The memorial site underscores the importance of preparation, caution and respect for these majestic mountains. The profound symbolism of Thukla Pass inspires and guides all on their trekking adventure to EBC!

Just another suspension bridge, all in a day's work😃!

*ANOTHER SUSPENSION BRIDGE...

*THE STORY OF HOW MT. EVEREST WAS CREATED

SOURCE: THE HISTORY CHANNEL *"How The Earth Was Made: Everest"*

Mount Everest was created by one of Earth's most dramatic and powerful geological events – the collision of two massive tectonic plates: the **Indian Plate** and the **Eurasian Plate.**

Around 200mm years ago, India wasn't connected to Asia – it was part of a giant southern supercontinent called Gondwana. Over millions of years, the Indian Plate began drifting northward across the Indian Ocean at a fast geological pace (15-20 cm per year).

Roughly 50mm years ago, India slammed into Asia. This wasn't a quick crash – it was a slow, grinding collision that's still occurring today at a rate of 5 cm per year. This caused the land to buckle and fold, giving rise to the **Himalayan mountain range,** including **Everest**.

Despite the destructive forces occurring today, associated with earthquakes and monsoons causing massive erosion, Everest is still growing a few millimeters each year.

CHAPTER NINE
*GORAKSHEP TREK (DAY 8)

Gorakshep is the highest overnight stop in the Everest Base Camp Trek and one day hike away from our destination of EBC. Trekking from Lobuche to Gorakshep was an adventure in itself. Gorakshep is also the last village in the Everest region. Therefore, you won't find a place to stay anywhere around the area besides this location.

> "
> *Mountain get out of my way!*
>
> -PAT H.

Taking a break along our trek to Gorak Shep! Our guide Ishwor is sitting on the rocks, bottom left with the bright yellow backpack, enjoying the beautiful, clear skies!

*THE LAST STOP BEFORE EBC...

📍**GORAKSHEP**
Small settlement in Nepal

*THE STORY OF BEAUTIFUL RACHEL

This tale is likely to get me in trouble, but the story must be told! Some would like to believe that she wasn't real, too perfect, a mirage, altitude sickness kicking in, possibly even an Everest Base Camp ghost. But for the team, she was real in every way, and just the motivation we all needed to finish our trek strong and get to our final destination – Everest Base Camp!

It all started mid-afternoon when we stopped at this teahouse to rest and have a hot cup of tea. The weather was clear, beautiful sunny day with a slight breeze. We sat on the far picnic table next to the building (highlighted in red below) to enjoy the solar heat coming off the building.

Beautiful Rachel

Then on the left side of the table, facing away from the building, but right in front of me sat **Beautiful Rachel**. Rachel had blonde hair, light skin, tall thin shape, wore a white sweater and black hiking pants, with boots and poles that, surprisingly, looked new. None of this would seem odd if she just started her trek, but what was fascinating, she just finished coming down from base camp that day. She was hiking alone with a single guide and she looked like she just spent the week at a spa! Of course, she took off her wool hat and it looked like she was at the hair dresser that morning, her hair shining, as she slowly flipped it back in the subtle breeze.

A common line used throughout the trek to get a conversation started was, "Hi, so where are you from," which I jumped on quickly! Rachel said she was from Amsterdam (definitely could hear the accent) and that's when we learned more about Rachel and her adventure.

After a nice conversation with this spectacular person (both inside and out), Rachel proceeded to get her gear and begin the trek back down the mountain. A few minutes after she left, I realized we never took a picture, how could we have missed that opportunity? Maybe because I got annoyed at a creepy guy at the table next to us taking a picture of Rachel from a distance, without her permission; not appropriate at all!

Rachel did mention that she writes a weekly blog, but we have been unsuccessful trying to locate her. Could Beautiful Rachel actually have been a figment of our imagination? The search continues!

*SUNNY DAYS & COLD NIGHTS

The last 3 days of the trek to base camp were beautiful, clear sunny days, not a cloud in the sky. This would change every day around 4:00pm as the clouds and fog would roll in, bringing brutally cold nights!!

*EVEREST BASE CAMP: ONLY A DAY AWAY...

Great pictures of the team stopping for a rest, having some protein bars and making sure we stay hydrated as we moved closer to our final destination: *Everest Base Camp*...one day away!

*THE VIEW FROM GORAKSHEP

View of Gorakshep as we descend into the village. Next stop: Everest Base Camp!
*Note the incredibly deep blue skies over snow capped mountains and rugged terrain.

*TYLER STRIKES AGAIN!

At the right time of day, generally early in the morning, the mountains would reflect the sun and turn the mountain peaks into this bright shade of gold. Truly beautiful if you can get out and tolerate the extremely cold conditions at this time of the day!

Tyler making sure she leaves **The Famous Parrot Lounge, Ft. Lauderdale** sticker on the top of the world for all to see!

This was the teahouse at **Gorakshep** just before it really got crowded with exhausted trekkers. Our room was down this dark hallway, which was exposed to the elements. This included the common bathroom at the end of the hall. Doorways were relatively short and I hit my head on the top of the bathroom doorframe numerous times in the middle of the night.

CHAPTER TEN

*EVEREST BASE CAMP – MISSION ACCOMPLISHED! (DAY 9)

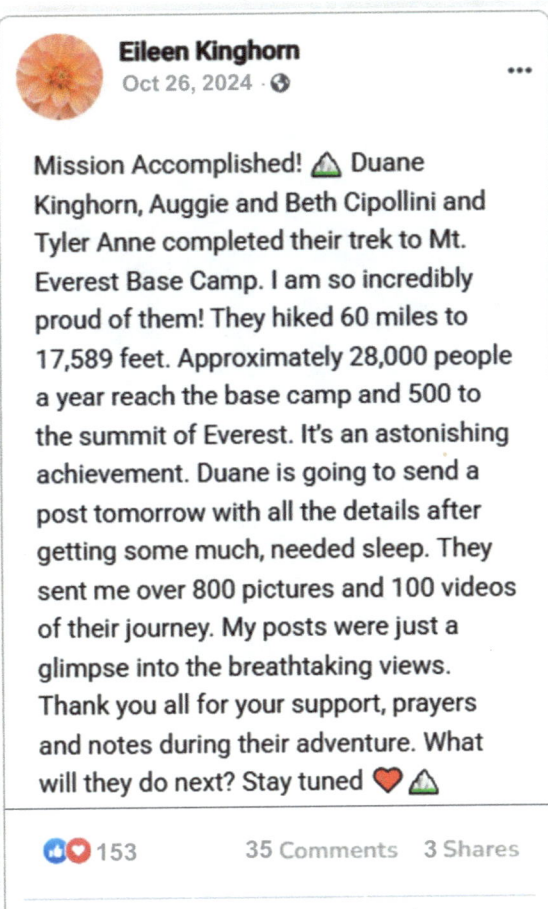

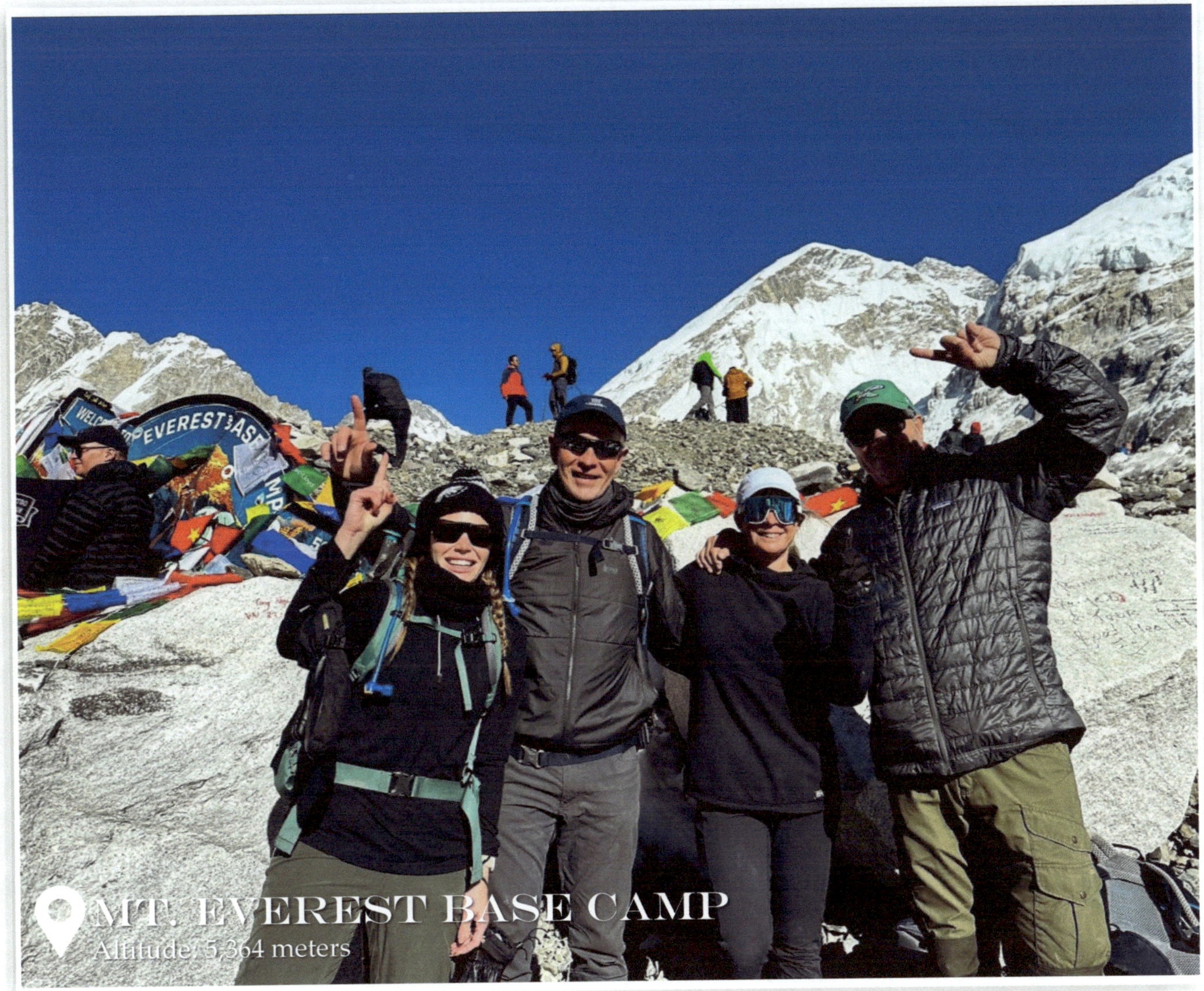
MT. EVEREST BASE CAMP
Altitude: 5,364 meters

Eileen Kinghorn
Oct 26, 2024 ·

Mission Accomplished! ⛰ Duane Kinghorn, Auggie and Beth Cipollini and Tyler Anne completed their trek to Mt. Everest Base Camp. I am so incredibly proud of them! They hiked 60 miles to 17,589 feet. Approximately 28,000 people a year reach the base camp and 500 to the summit of Everest. It's an astonishing achievement. Duane is going to send a post tomorrow with all the details after getting some much, needed sleep. They sent me over 800 pictures and 100 videos of their journey. My posts were just a glimpse into the breathtaking views. Thank you all for your support, prayers and notes during their adventure. What will they do next? Stay tuned ❤️ ⛰

153 35 Comments 3 Shares

Like Comment Share

FACEBOOK POST
Eileen Kinghorn, Oct. 26, 2024

*THESE MAGNIFICENT MOUNTAINS

"
Beautiful pictures.
Stunning!

-DONNA F.

Although these pictures are amazing, I wish there was a more creative way to capture the massive size and scale of these mountains! The Team all agreed: you need to experience in person to fully appreciate the sheer magnitude and beauty!

As we moved closer to base camp in the higher elevations, the terrain was more rugged and as these pictures reflect, with us wearing warmer clothing, much colder. The views of the sun shinning on the snow-capped mountains was out of this world!! We had to stop ourselves along the way to take it all in and realize where we were and what we were doing!

"

Simply incredible Duane Kinghorn! Congratulations on this wonderful life experience!

-OMAR J.

"

Omg a frigging mazing!

-IRENE R.

*THE EBC DREAM TEAM!

AUGGIE, TYLER AND BETH CIPOLLINI, DUANE KINGHORN, ISHWOR & SANKE

> "
> *Congrats Duane. What an accomplishment! The pictures were so beautiful. Thanks so much for sharing your experience with us. Loved!*
>
> -SUE W.

"
That's one cool Dad. Nice job Pops!
-MATT P.

EVEREST BASE CAMP – MISSION ACCOMPLISHED! (DAY 9)

*ADVENTURE OF A LIFETIME

We couldn't have done this adventure without our main man **Sanke** and this amazing team...**Tyler, Beth and Auggie**! So much fun and support – the two weeks went by so quickly and the adventure already seems like a lifetime ago! We are still contemplating what our next escapade will be...knowing Beth and Auggie, they have something up their sleeves!

*SHOUT OUT TO PROCARE

My friends at **ProCare Rehabilitation** made this excursion possible. After completely tearing my rectus femoris tendon in my left leg during a race, I spent a year of physical therapy at ProCare. Big thank you to my therapist Guiliana! When Steve Friedman (owner), I think, jokingly suggested carrying the ProCare banner to Everest, I said, "of course I would! Let's do it! Why not?" I probably surprised Steve with my response, the least I could do!

> **"**
> *Congratulations Duane.*
> *You're an amazing man.*
> *Onto the next challenge!!*
>
> -STEVE F.

*A MISSION OF LOVE

Happy to support my neighbor Kathy Majewski and her brother Owen Bradley on spreading their mission of **Love** across the globe!

The day before we reached Mount Everest, Kathy informed Eileen that Owen had just received a call that a lung transplant donor was identified for Owen. The next day he received a double lung transplant – his and the prayers of many came true!

"

*Grateful to our neighbor, Duane Kinghorn, for carrying and sharing **Orbit of Love** — all the way from VT to NJ to Kathmandu on his journey to Mount Everest.*

-KATHY BRADLEY MAJEWSKI

> " *Duane Because it was there Kinghorn. Beyond amazed, my friend. Congratulations!*
>
> -AJAY D.

*SHOUT OUT TO THE PARROT

Tyler showing support for their favorite Fort Lauderdale local hangout by leaving the Parrot Lounge decal across the world. **The Famous Parrot** has been serving Fort Lauderdale locals and visitors since 1970. The Parrot offers a friendly neighborhood atmosphere with friendly service and good food and libations!

PARROT LOUNGE®
911 Sunrise Ln
Ft. Lauderdale, FL

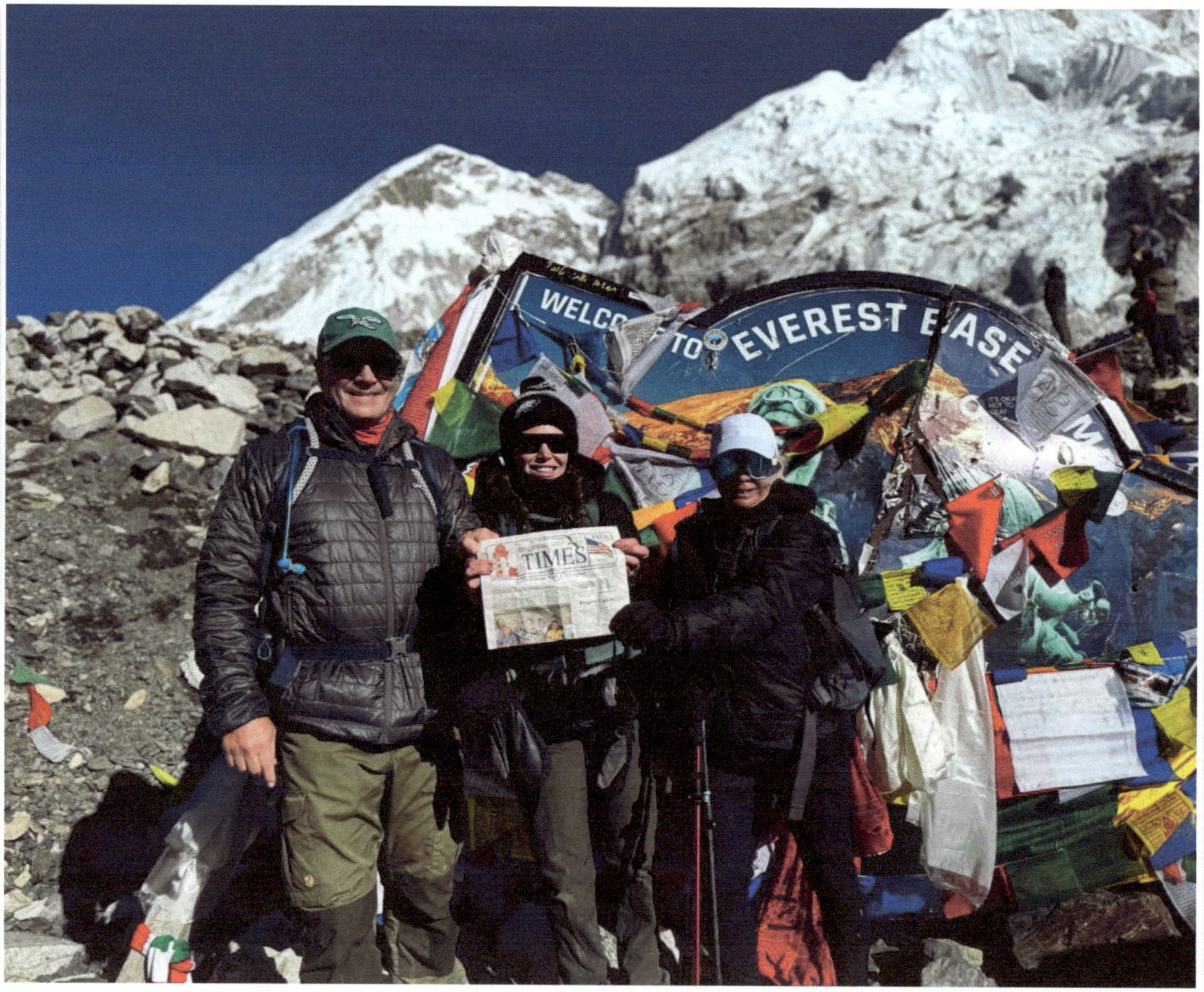

After completion of our trek to Everest Base Camp, we returned to Gorakshep for one last freezing night! There are no teahouses in the Everest Base Camp area, nor are trekkers allowed to camp there.

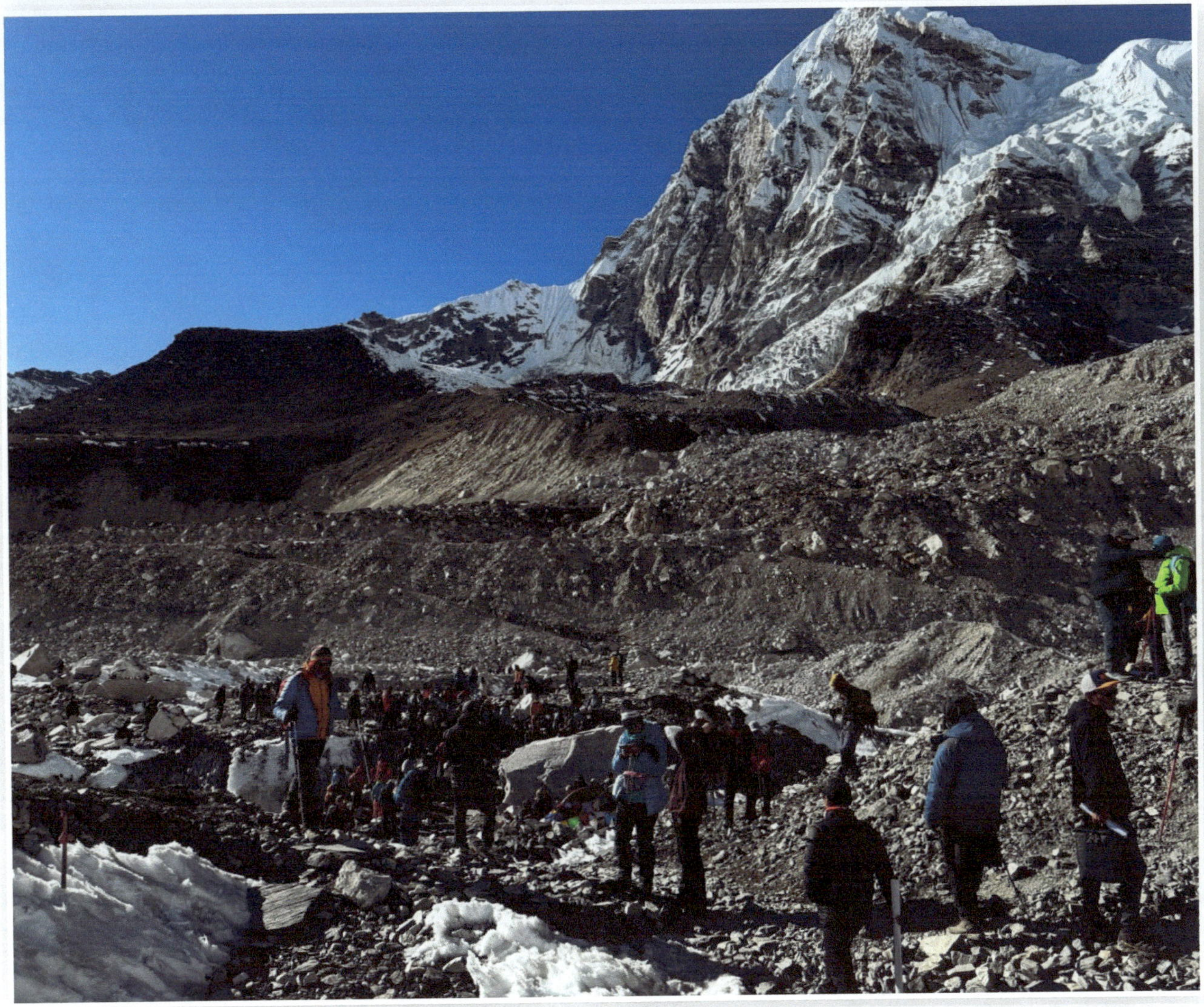

GORAKSHEP

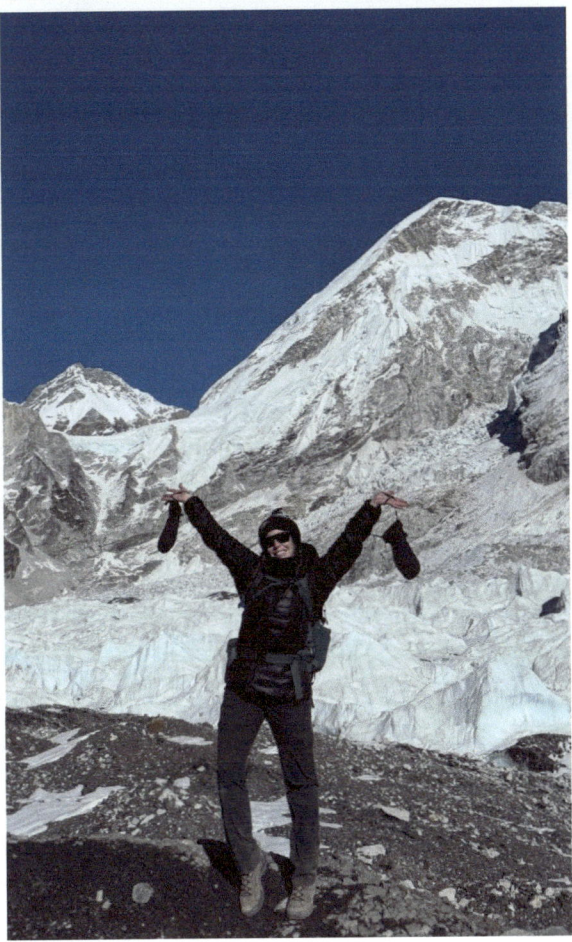

*SIZE CONSTANCY

The team is standing at approx. 18,000 feet (EBC), while the peak of Mount Everest in the background (over Tyler's left shoulder) is at 29,000 feet.

There are several reasons for this photography phenomena, which render large objects small or small objects large. The primary cause being "Size Constancy," where in the real world, the eye and brain automatically adjust the retinal image.

For example, a stop sign on a 6' pole looks like a stop sign atop a 6' pole, regardless of how far down the road you are. We are familiar with the common stop sign (as well as other general standards for road signs that create this consistency), so our brain assigns a size constancy to that familiar object.

Many of us, regardless of our photographic experience, have stood in awe, before a scenic landscape of a spectacular mountain range (e.g. Mount Everest), and have then been disappointed when seeing the miniature print of the photograph we took. The mountains looked so much larger to the naked eye! *Size constancy*.

EVEREST BASE CAMP — MISSION ACCOMPLISHED! (DAY 9)

129

*EVEREST BASE CAMP: WE MADE IT!

The team shares a celebratory group hug at Everest Base Camp – full of emotion and incredibly proud of our accomplishment!!

*ALTITUDE ADJUSTMENT REACHED

> **"**
>
> *Grateful Mission Accomplished! My Dad and Team made it to Mount Everest base camp after a long couple weeks of hiking and braving the elements with very little training. I still think he's insane, but what an experience, such a cool journey... Crazy ✅, Amazing ✅!*
>
> -RYAN K.

CHAPTER ELEVEN
*RETURN TRIP FROM GORAKSHEP
TO KATHMANDU (DAY 10)

We took three helicopter rides to get back to Kathmandu. We waited over 3 hours on a steep mountain at Gorakshep for a helicopter, which was delayed due to rescue missions at base camp, they always take priority.

The first flight out of **Gorakshep**, was a short 5-minute flight to a landing pad in a remote area known as **Pheriche**. There were weight limits that required us to split up the team and take separate flights into Pheriche. Beth and I took the first flight and Auggie and Tyler took the second, arriving 20 minutes after us. This video includes Beth and I boarding the helicopter and leaving Gorakshep, the first leg of our long trip home!

From there we all were able to take the next flight together into **Lukla**. Unfortunately, the next flight from Lukla to **Kathmandu** was delayed a couple hours due to poor weather conditions, clouds and fog had quickly rolled in. When there was a slight break in the weather and although the conditions were poor, they opened the heliport, but only for a short window, which allowed us to get out. Once we were 5 minutes out of Lukla, the weather cleared enough to at least give us visual site of the mountains, taking us approx. 40 minutes to arrive at Kathmandu.

📍GORAKSHEP 🚁 PHERICHE 🚁 LUKLA 🚁 KATHMANDU

*SURREAL VIDEOS OF OUR HELICOPTER FLIGHT
From Gorakshep to Perhiche

*TREKKING BACKWARDS

Auggie and Tyler flying into Perhiche, from Gorakshep, meeting up with Beth and I for our next helicopter flight into Lukla.

" *This is the most amazing thing I've ever seen!*

-KAREN E.

*WAIT. REST. TRAVEL.

During our 3 hour wait for a helicopter, Tyler found a comfortable rock in the bright sun to catch up on some reading. Once we were ready to go, you can see Beth waving good-bye from inside our helicopter.

*LAST CALL FOR CHALLENGES

> " *Amazing journey! Congratulations for completing such an incredible challenge and for sharing it with us.*
>
> -MARY G.

While we were waiting for our helicopter out of Gorakshep, we took a picture of me on the landing pad to give some context to how small it was – no room for error here!! Also, we had to climb this steep mountain to get to it.

*INCLEMENT WEATHER CHANGES

Lukla: when we landed (beautiful skies) and later when we took off in the dense fog. That was absolutely frightening and out of my comfort zone for sure!

LUKLA

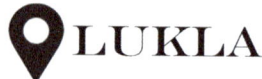

Planes and helicopters taking off at **Lukla**, considered to be one of the most dangerous airports in the world! You can see how the clouds started to roll in and within 30 minutes you couldn't see the end of the heliport or runway.

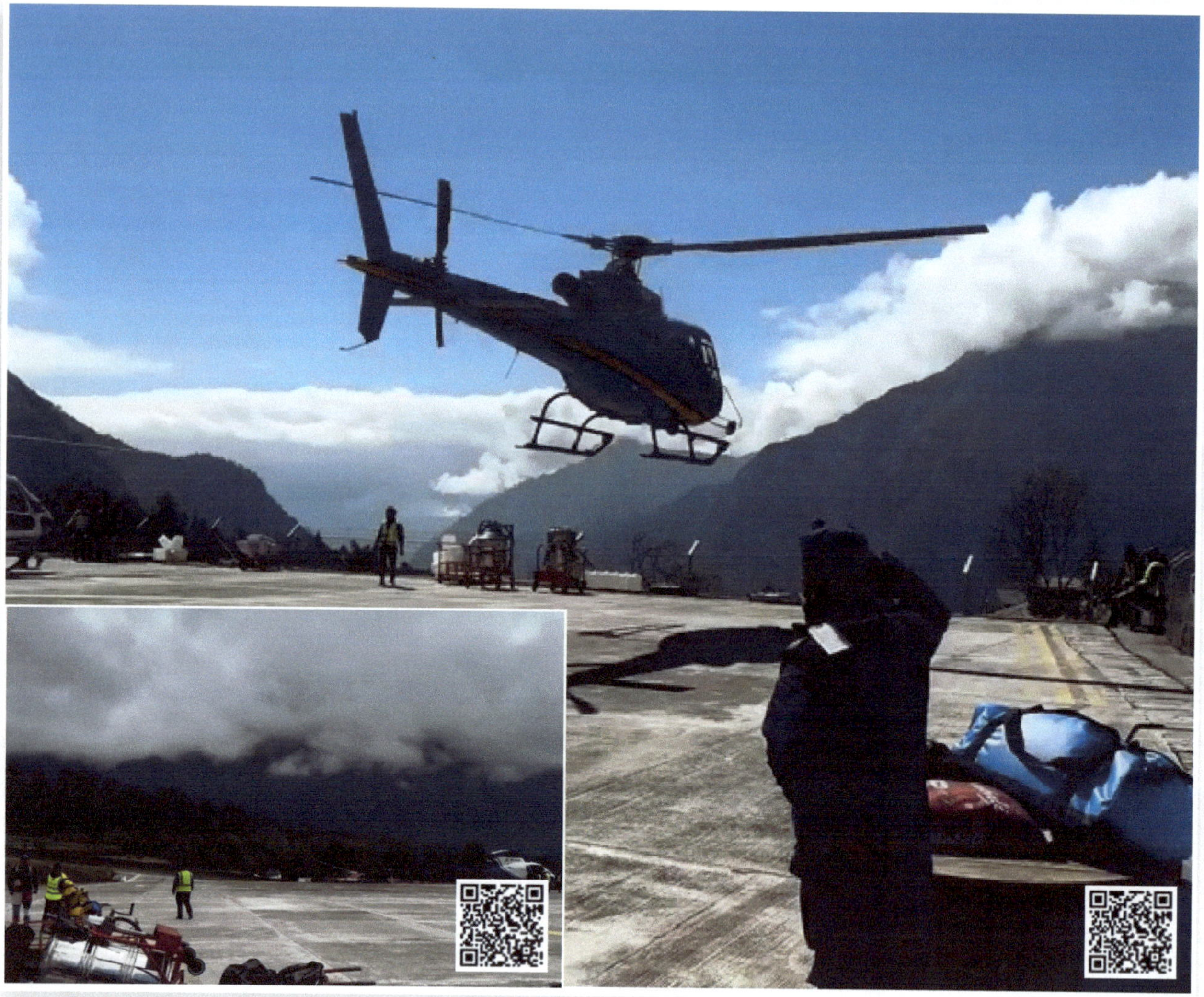

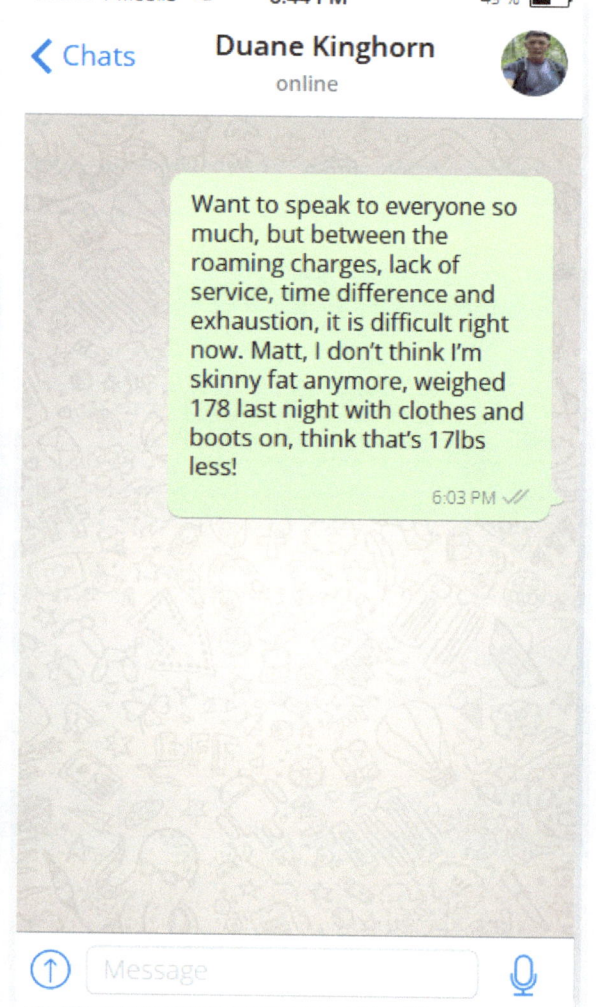

●●●○○ T-Mobile 4G
6:44 PM
49 %
Chats
Duane Kinghorn
online
Want to speak to everyone so much, but between the roaming charges, lack of service, time difference and exhaustion, it is difficult right now. Matt, I don't think I'm skinny fat anymore, weighed 178 last night with clothes and boots on, think that's 17lbs less!
6:03 PM
Message

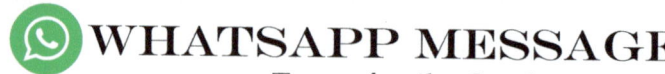

WHATSAPP MESSAGE
To my family, October 26, 2024

*MOUNT EVEREST: CRUSHED!

...We conquered **MOUNT EVEREST BASE CAMP** and all our fears, now we are heading back to Kathmandu to celebrate our adventure with our new friends from Magnificent Himalayan Treks! Where's Tyler? – she took over co-piloting duties and is enjoying the ride in the front seat!

*TYLER THE CO-PILOT

Tyler in the co-pilot seat and loving every minute! Me? I was just as happy in my middle aisle seat right behind her!

*BACK TO KATHMANDU

Amazing helicopter videos as we approached **Kathmandu**!

CHAPTER TWELVE

*EVEREST BASE CAMP ADVENTURE ENDS

First thing we did when we got back was have lunch at a nice restaurant in Kathmandu and I enjoyed my first ice coffee in 2 weeks! If you look closely, you can see the scab on my left elbow, where I leaned into a boulder during the first 5 minutes of our trek day 1! I was 17lbs. lighter in this picture, with Auggie losing 14lbs.

Victory Dinner: the team heading out to celebrate.

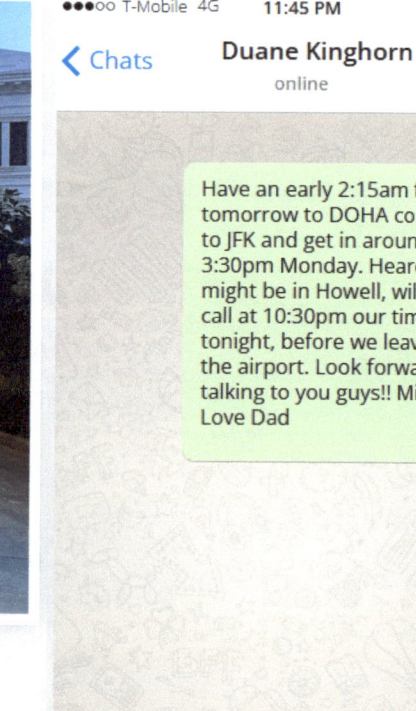

> **"**
> *Here's to an even bigger 2025 for you (maybe we stop climbing mountains, though we were worried for a bit there). Love you Dad.*
>
> -MATT K.

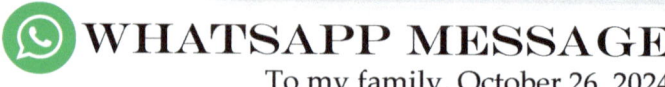 **WHATSAPP MESSAGE**
To my family, October 26, 2024

The team enjoying a wonderful dinner celebration at the beautiful **Hotel Barahi** rooftop restaurant in downtown Kathmandu! The event was hosted by Bhim Panta and the amazing team at Magnificent Himalayas Trek, including our friends Sanke and Manit who joined the celebration!

📍 NARAYANHITI PALACE
History Museum, Kathmandu, Nepal

The **Narayanhiti Palace**, former home of the royal family: Following the abolishment of the monarchy on May 28, 2008, the building and its grounds have been turned into a museum.

📍 HOTEL BARAHI
Pokhara Valley, Nepal

*STUNNING VIEWS FROM ABOVE

Overlooking Downtown Kathmandu

The **Nepalese Royal Massacre** occurred on June 1, 2001 at the Narayanhiti Palace, the then-residence of the Nepali monarchy. Nine members of the royal family, including King Birendra and Queen Aishwarya, were killed in a mass shooting during a gathering of the royal family at the palace. A government-appointed inquiry team named Crown Prince Dipendra as perpetrator of the massacre. Dipendra slipped into a coma after shooting himself in the head.

Despite his role in the massacre, Dipendra was declared King of Nepal while comatose after murdering his father and brothers. He died in the hospital three days after the massacre without regaining consciousness. Birendra's brother, Gyanendra then became king.

SOURCE: WIKIPEDIA, The Free Encyclopedia, Nepalese Royal Massacre

Nepalese Royal Massacre

EVEREST BASE CAMP ADVENTURE ENDS

*LIFE IMITATES ART. ART IMITATES LIFE.

When we got back to Kathmandu, after conquering all our fears climbing to Mount Everest Base Camp, we had some time to experience the local culture and explore the city. That included visiting various art galleries and seeing works from local artists. Each of us purchased an original art piece to remember our adventure. Watching Auggie, the master negotiator in action was priceless. Not only was it entertaining, but we definitely got the best deals!! This was mine, which I had framed and matted when we returned home.

*TRAVELING BACK TO REALITY

DOHA, QATAR
Capital city, Persian Gulf Coast

Heading to **Kathmandu Tribhuvan International Airport**, where we traveled to Doha, Qatar. After a short layover with the team in Doha, we were off to the US, where I flew back to New York and Beth, Auggie and Tyler to Ft. Lauderdale.

*LASTING SYMBOLS OF FRIENDSHIP

The yellow scarfs were a **symbol of friendship** given to us by our host Bhim Panta, we were so appreciative of the entire team's support and hospitality! These were genuinely some of the nicest people we've ever met, and will be friends for life!

During our wait in line, the man with the yellow and red outfit below (also had bright green pants), recognized that we were Americans and started to heckle us regarding the upcoming US elections. He was from Germany. He was clearly not a Trump fan, and made it well known. We took it all in stride, but as Americans do, we made sure we had the last laugh – will leave that story for Auggie to share!

*WAIT. REFLECT. REST. TRAVEL.

A three-hour layover at the Doha Qatar **Hamad International Airport**, allowed us some time to relive the AMAZING last two weeks, rest and visit these breathtaking gardens in the center of the airport!

⚲HAMAD INTERNATIONAL AIRPORT
Doha, Qatar

FINAL THOUGHTS

What an amazing trip, will remember every minute from the time my good friend Irene dropped me off at the Atlantic City International Airport, to when Michael picked me up at JFK Airport and took me to Roll N Roaster for this incredible roast beef sandwich – they are truly the best of friends!!

When planning this trip, I realized quickly that I really didn't fully understand what I was getting into, that is an understatement! But I did know for sure that I was undertaking this journey with the most genuine and likeable people you would ever meet: the Cipollinis! Regardless, living with someone is different then occasionally hanging out. You wonder how will you get along being with the same group 24x7, every day for 3 weeks straight? Will they appreciate your sense of humor, bathroom habits, will you get on each others nerves, will there be disagreements, etc.?

Of course there was none of that with this group, we laughed every day! There was no drama or conflicts of any kind, to the contrary, only support for each other, fun, flexibility, positivity, friendship, openness and honesty! This turned out to be a **Trip of a Lifetime** in every way, that we will all cherish and remember forever!!

Beth, Auggie and Tyler, thank you for allowing me to be part of this special adventure with you, always making me feel like I was part of the family!! So grateful to have had this opportunity, looking forward to our next expedition!

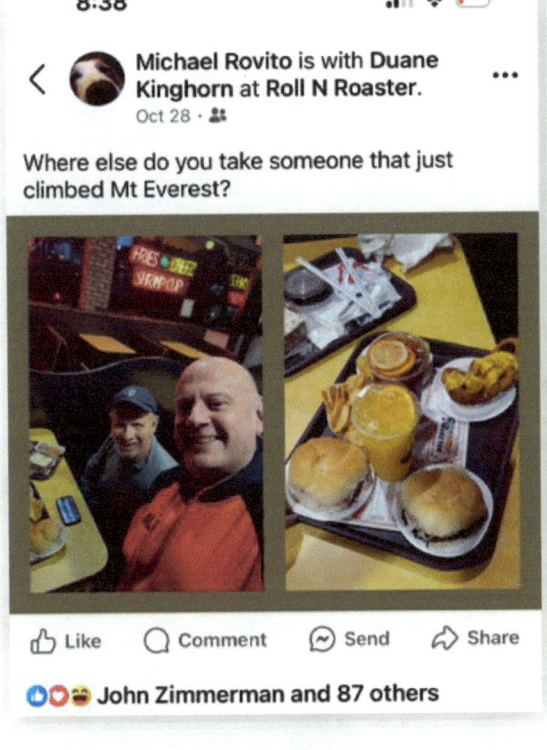

> ❝
> *Wow you guys are brave!!! But it's got to be entertaining with Beth and Auggie!!! LOL*
>
> –BETTINA E.

> ❝
> *Haha roll n roaster is the best. You went from Mt Everest to Brooklyn!*
>
> –LORI B.

Duane Kinghorn
3h · 🌐

I am not much of a social media guy, so thank you for allowing me to share this experience with you one more time 😎! Also thank you all for watching the journey, your messages, motivating us and sending your best wishes and prayers, I can't begin to tell you how inspiring it was!! All of you do such amazing things every day and for me this was just an opportunity to see how far I could push my limits and persevere through all the challenges and obstacles that were thrown at us, and there were a few 🧗. Show less

❤️👍 157   49 Comments 15 Shares

👍 Like   💬 Comment   ↪ Share

Duane Kinghorn
3h · 🌐

Ever since I retired, I felt there was much more out there to experience, so why not go to Mount Everest 😄! Here in Kathmandu, we were all just discussing how hard it is to explain this experience, from the incredible views we saw everywhere, every day, to pushing yourself physically to the limits and ultimately overcoming those fears of what's ahead.

The weather conditions for the most part were perfect during the day, but at night it was a completely different story! When the sun went down, it felt like you were sometimes sleeping on ice, even fully clothed for the next day, wrapped in sleeping bag with liners! I will save you all from the different bathroom experiences, you can read that one in Augie's book 😆. Show less

❤️👍 157   49 Comments 15 Shares

👍 Like   💬 Comment   ↪ Share

Duane Kinghorn
3h · 🌐

It was also fun meeting people along the way from all over the world, listening to their stories and experiences. Places like Amsterdam, Nepal, Canada, Switzerland, Iran, India, Vietnam, Taiwan, Croatia, France, England, Australia and so many more.

As Eileen mentioned we hiked 60 miles over 7 days, to 17,600 feet. I kept hearing this would be life changing and for me, reaching base camp did bring me closer to the family members and friends I miss the most!

Finally, in addition to all of you, thank you to Beth, Auggie and Tyler for allowing me to take this journey with you, no better team❤️! Show less

❤️👍 157   49 Comments 15 Shares

👍 Like   💬 Comment   ↪ Share

f

FACEBOOK POST
Duane Kinghorn, Oct. 27, 2024

EVEREST BASE CAMP ADVENTURE ENDS

Enjoy!!! You got this DK!!!

Welcome to Nepal It's going to be epic. Safe travels Stay safe

Wow! Amazing! Good Luck!!! Awesome Enjoy!!!

Fabulous!!! Good luck!!! Good Luck!!! Awesome Enjoy!!! Be safe DK Quite adventure!!

Stay safe Duane! Go Duane Go! Great shots Duane Keep Chugging along!!!

You are so brave, what an experience! You have this!! Good luck and be safe!

The smiles tell it all. Enjoyment of the experience! Wish you all well and good health for the climb!!!

Great picture safe journey Awesome Duane. Stay safe!! Totally awesome! What an adventure. Be safe and enjoy!!

This looks amazing!!! Be careful!!! What an adventure! Duane, thank you for sharing this amazing experience with us!

So excited ING have a wonderful time stay safe Wow! Enjoy the adventure! Wow, breathtaking pictures! Good luck with the next leg and stay safe.

Looks amazing !! I'm loving all the pictures!!Amazing Enjoy the adventure! Wow!! That is absolutely amazing! Good Luck to them on this incredible journey!

Love all the pictures Good luck ..you've got this. Such an amazing experience Sounds like an incredible experience so far. You are a far braver man than I would ever be!!

You got this!! So impressive! Looks absolutely amazing! So amazing, Duane... as long as you stay safe! You are much braver than I am, that's for sure! Wow!

Wow, good for u guys! Only 6k mgore feet to go! Good luck! This is amazing. I am pretty sure I would be passed out at that altitude. Just Wow! Amazing! Stay safe!!

Good luck Duane. What an incredible adventure. Amazing I'm so proud of you! I love seeing the pictures and admire their courage but definitely not on my bucket list!!!

That is a beautiful chunk of earth...enjoy Incredible!!! Be safe Thank you for the posts. Must be a wonderful experience but a message Wow love seeing this journey beautiful!!!

Amazing pictures ... great trip Beautiful scenery!! Go DK and team! Amazing! from my mom and me to my brother, sister-in-law, and niece... God Bless, Very Courageous and Adventurous, WTG Wow!

Incredible journey! Thanks for sharing, Eileen! This is great!! Make this the last out of country excursion. There is so much to Amazing Duane...stay safe Ggooo DUANE. Up Gogo Up.

Wow! Absolutely wonderful pictures! Just WOW Amazing pictures!! see in the good 'ole united states. YOU MAKE US TOO NERVOUS Wow fantastic pictures. Safe journey home Amazing!

Great pics! Wow Totally Awesome Amazing Duane! Keep ascending with these far away places. Had a great time showing you around! Hope you're ready for what's next! Looks amazing

Wow!! You can do it Duane (and team)! Wow! Beth Cipollini you are amazing! What an accomplishment. I'm enjoying watching your journey. Definitely bucket list material, Travel safe Duane.

Thanks for sharing this incredible adventure! Was on my bucket list but now unless it's by plane I'll never get to it so living vicariously through you! Wow, fantastic pix! Keep on truckin Duane...

Wow truly amazing Duane! What is the temperature now? Great pictures! Stay safe on this trip of a lifetime Amazing! You are a rockstar! Keep on trekking This looks amazing Just amazing!

Beautiful! Gorgeous pictures!! Enjoy every minute of it!! Congrats Duane. Wish I could do what you just experienced its a chance of a lifetime, most important, you're back safe welcome back!

Stunning pictures! Sending prayers and good thoughts for a successful hike to Dingboche! Looks amazing and the weather seems to be perfect. One step at a time You didn't hit the pick 6 pool

Questions how heavy is your pack? Do you camp at night or stay inside? Love the pics! Congrats! Absolutely breathtaking! Go Gogo Kinghorn teamThe Jets lost 37-15. Great views! Amazing

wow, so exciting. thanks for taking us along on the journey. Was there a lot of training before Duane could go on this trip of a life time? Pictures are just breathtaking!! This is great! Fantastic!!!

Totally awesome Breathtaking!!! Thanks for the update, Eileen. Keep up the great work all of you!

Awesome Duane. Enjoy the adventures! Can't wait to hear the stories Wow! Super cool!

Omg! What an amazing g experience! Fantastic photos! Thank you be safe! Great pictures. Enjoy!

*MESSAGE OF GRATITUDE:

A huge thank you to everyone that followed our journey and sent such inspiring messages of encouragement!

Awesome Duane. Stay safe!! Wow, good for u guys! Only 6k more feet to go! Good luck! Stay safe Duane! Stay safe God Bless, Very Courageous and Adventurous, WTG

So, so amazing!!!Some of my very best friends are on the same trek right now! Wow Duane! Yes crazy, but inspiring! Looking forward to following your adventure!

This is amazing!!! Beautiful pictures Wow! Beautiful pictures. Safe travels to Duane and his crew. Stay safe and can't wait to hear all the stories of this journey.

Oh wow! How cool. That's a hard no for me and the suspension bridges! Oh my! Best of luck to them! Amazing adventure! Praying for their safe return!

OMG! Nope not me on that bridge. Can't wait for more pictures and he's stories when he comes back. Wow, how amazing!!! Amazing pictures.

Good luck and I'm looking forward to following this adventure of yours!! Wow! So excited for them! Amazing ! Safe journey! Go Duane!

Really cool looking trip   Be safe Duane.. this is amazing! Very proud of you !!! This is so awesome I can't wait to hear all about it !!

Wow! Sounds like a great adventure! Good luck and safe travels! DK! This is amazing! I can't wait to follow along! Safe travels!

What awesome photos! Enjoy every moment! Loved Kathmandu. Great to see it again through your eyes. Enjoy the trek.

Great update. Thanks Duane and wishing you the best. Be safe. We missed you at the Army Ten Miler, but you will

OMG please stay safe, we need you in our piece here in NJ   love your hiking!!! The runners are still sleeping.

Wow! Sending good vibes, prayers and everything else that first with it!Awesome, be safe and ENJOY!!

I went there years ago! Hope you're acclimating to Looks like a bucket-list adventure, good luck!

the altitude and the smell of yak butter Good luck Have a great time. Be safe Safe Travels

The messages kept on coming — Thank you!

Wow. Sounds awesome....enjoy every step ...I'm guessing there   Do they have Pork Roll?

will be lots of them. Looking forward to seeing your pictures. Awesome Hydrate and stay safe

I love that you will be sharing your journey along the way. Go   Good luck, safe travels and have fun!

Duane!! (and team) stay safe!! Godspeed, my friend! What an amazing adventure you'll have! Good Luck

Wow, quite the adventure. Good luck with the rest of your climb!! What did you eat for lunch? This is awesome

We miss you already...So impressed you're Thanks for any news Would love to be there but it was never on my agenda

doing this! Be safe and keep us all posted!   What everyone else said madness what the heck. see you in base camp South

Wow. So amazing. Looking forward to following adventure. Be safe! Wowza!!!super excited to see you on this trip!!! Safe travels

Duane - amazing pictures! Go DK and team!   What an amazing adventure of a lifetime. Stay safe, stay present and enjoy the journey!

You are amazing Duane!! How inspiring (and yes, utterly insane!) you are! I can't wait to followYou got this DK!! God4will watchtower them.

your travels and wish you safe journey my friend. Get back SAFELY so we can all have a drink and listen   Amazing pictures! So glad they made it!

to the amazing stories you will have to tell. Wow! What an amazing experience. Saying prayers for a successful and safe journey. Quite adventure!!Wow!

Great photos!! Go Duane (and team) go!! Omg! That's incredible you could never find me doing that! Omg a frigging mazing! All the best! Can't wait for pics!

Wow, this is awesome and exciting! I can't wait to see the next post! Enjoy and be safe, my friend! Good luck Duane!   What a great adventure !! It's going to be epic.

Sounds like an incredible experience so far. You are a far braver man than I would ever be!! You have this!! Good luck and be safe! Wow!!! Awesome! Amazing! Stay safe!!

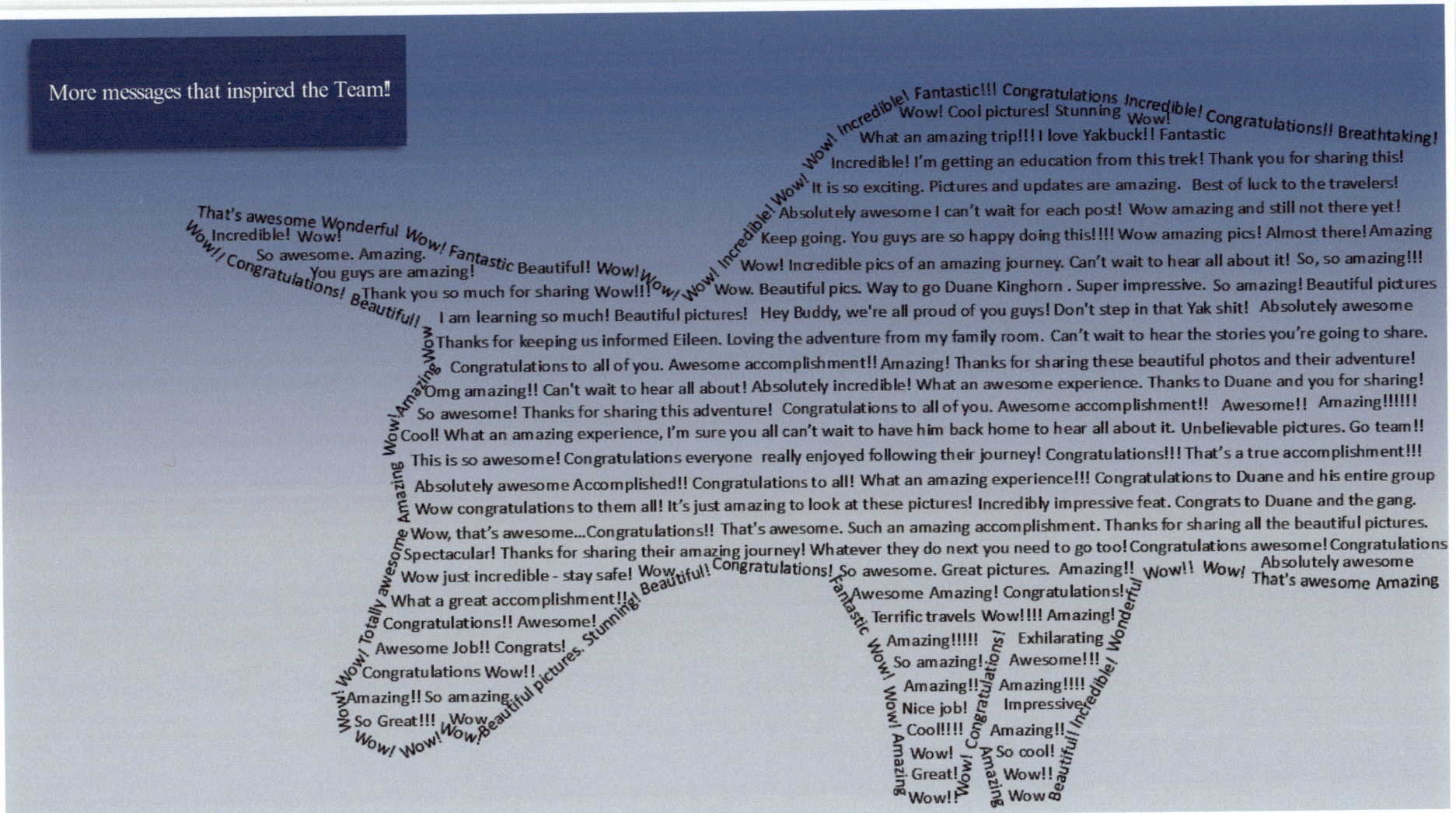

Wonderful!! So Cool! Way to go Duane! Wow Congrats Amazing Wow Awesome! Wow Wow Wow! Amazing Cool! Wow So very cool!!! Congratulations Duane! Amazing Wow Wow, Just Wow

Wow Wow! Wow Stunning Congratulations So cool Duane Wow So Cool! Wow Fantastic Wow Amazing! Just amazing! Beautiful Congrats. Amazing accomplishment. Wow So awesome Duane!!

Congratulations what an experience Congratulations to then! So impressive! Congratulations!! Pictures are so beautiful! Wow Wow Amazing journey! Congrats!

Congratulations to Duane!!!! That's awesome Duane!! What an experience, Duane! What a great accomplishment. Inspiring Congratulations Absolutely Amazing

Beautiful thanks for sharing! Absolutely stunning!! Congratulations to Duane!! Amazing!!!! Congratulations to you and your team! Such an amazing experience for you!

Congratulations to the team! Incredible accomplishment! Congratulations awesome job Awesome accomplishment! Congratulations!

Wow! Stunning! I loved following you! Great job Duane!! A trip you'll never forget!!!!! Awesome experience!! Awesome!! Way to go Duane! Wow! That is awesome! A great accomplishment!

So Cool!!!! Gorgeous! Congratulations great accomplishment! Sounds amazing!! What an achievement! Beautiful!! Congratulations!! Amazing! Congratulations! What an amazing accomplishment!

Congratulations! Gorgeous! So Congratulations pictures are so beautiful. Wow Absolutely amazing!! Congratulations You should feel very proud for what you accomplished!

Very cool Duane!! Absolutely stunning! This is the most amazing thing I've ever seen! Awesome Wow Wow! This is the most amazing thing I've ever seen! Truly amazing!!!

This sounds amazing! Cool Wow Cool!! Congratulations to then! So impressive! Beautiful!! Stunning trek!!! Wow Stunning! What a great accomplishment. Congratulations!! A M A Z I N G!!!

Congrats to all of you!! Wow Amazing! Just amazing! Stunning! Cool!!! Gorgeous! Amazing Awesome Duane! Wow Stunning Congratulations to the team! Incredible accomplishment!

What an accomplishment Beautiful!! Wow!! Congratulations!! Gorgeous Congratulations Team Wow The photos are spectacular! Amazing accomplishment

What an awesome experience!!! Wow Amazing stunning! Amazing!!!! Awesome! So cool! Wow Wow Absolutely amazing Duane! Great! Wonderful!! Such an amazing journey! Congratulations!! Pictures are so beautiful! Congratulations

Great journey Duane. I looked into the Everest Base Camp treks more than a few times. Congratulations! Such an amazing accomplishment. Loved seeing this journey life changer!

Congratulations to Duane and his team. What a great accomplishment. thanks for sharing your journey with all of us. So proud of you Love from here! Lifetime experience!!

This is such an accomplishment! Way to go Duane and fellow climbers. Can't wait to see more! Absolutely amazing! Congratulations Duane and crew! Blessed travels back home!

What an incredible experience! I loved just following along! Congratulations to Duane and his amazing team! Amazing pictures of what looks like a once in a lifetime journey!!

Awesome pictures! Please know that we are so proud of you. You did something I know I would never do. Now come back safely and go play some golf with Matt. Impressive!

EVEREST BASE CAMP ADVENTURE ENDS

EPILOGUE

The only thing I ever did as crazy as trekking to **Mount Everest Base Camp**, was jumping out of a plane, **sky diving!!** They were two epic accomplishments—ticking off two wildly different but equally exhilarating dreams from life's adventure bucket list ⛰️ 🪂!

From Peaks to Plummets: A Tale of Two Adrenalines

Some adventures whisper through the wind, others roar through your veins. Trekking to Everest Base Camp and skydiving couldn't be more different—and yet somehow, they both tugged at the same corner of my soul: the one that craves awe, fear, and adventure.

Trekking to Everest Base Camp is a slow-burn triumph: altitude pushing your limits, oxygen playing hard to get, and every step demanding focus and confidence. It was a challenge that unfolded with each sunrise—a test of endurance! It's the kind of crazy that builds with time, where your strength is revealed little by little. That first glimpse of the towering peaks, the prayer flags fluttering in the wind—it's soul-stirring. Standing at Base Camp, I didn't feel triumphant. I felt small, quiet, and deeply alive.

Skydiving, on the other hand, is a jolt of adrenaline in the span of a few breathtaking minutes, a burst! It's raw, loud, and fast. A single inhale, a leap, and gravity vanished. Noise became silence. My heart raced to catch up with my body as it plummeted through a canvas of clouds. It was terrifying. It was euphoric. It was over in minutes, a controlled chaos of thrill, defiance of gravity, and trust in your gear and your courage.

But this wasn't just any skydive—it was "Jump for Jo." My sister, Jo, was battling Leukemia at the time, and I turned my leap into a fundraiser to support her fight. The jump wasn't just about adrenaline; it was about hope, love, and the power of showing up for someone you care about!

And here's the twist: I wasn't alone. I jumped out of that plane with someone I'd met on a bus just three months earlier. A stranger turned co-adventurer, their presence added an unexpected layer of camaraderie and spontaneity to the experience. Today, that stranger (Pete) is a close friend—a bond forged in freefall and strengthened by shared adventure. Also, Pete is a Leukemia survivor, 12 years after we jumped out of a plane together, he was diagnosed with stage 4 Leukemia, and I'm happy to say has beat this dreadful disease and is doing well today!

The contrast is poetic—Everest humbles you gradually, skydiving humbles you instantly. Everest was earned mile by mile, and skydiving was about surrendering to the moment.

The Everest trek was a slow crescendo. Days of relentless hiking, the weight of altitude pressing on every breath, and the surreal beauty of ice giants watching from above. Everest taught me patience, persistence, and the beauty of gradual achievement. Skydiving taught me to let go. Together, they stitched a story across my life—one that says: I showed up for the climb, and I didn't flinch for the fall.

*EVEREST: MISSION ACCOMPLISHED!

EVEREST BASE CAMP ADVENTURE ENDS

*EVEREST BASE CAMP EXPEDITION
OCTOBER 14-31, 2024

DHANYABAD!

TO THE EDGE OF EVEREST

www.ingramcontent.com/pod-product-compliance
Lightning Source LLC
Chambersburg PA
CBHW040812120626

46547CB00004B/524